Ogham:
The Secret Language of the Druids

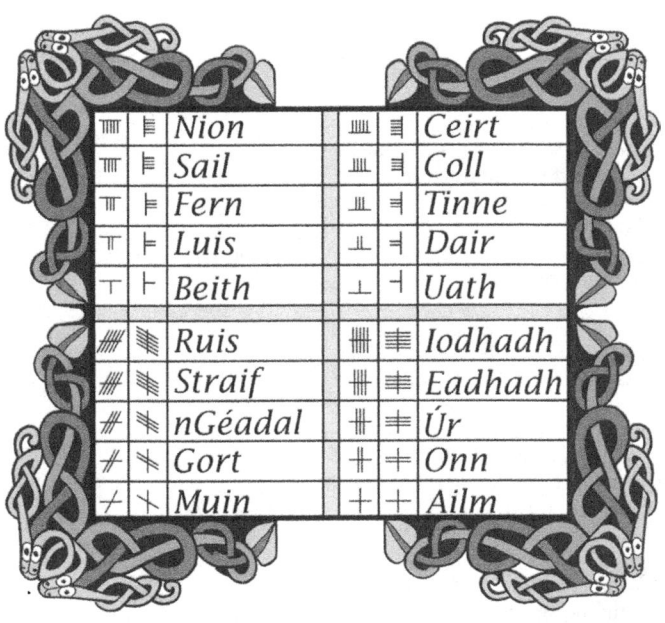

Rev. Robert Lee "Skip" Ellison
Archdruid-Ár nDraíocht Féin (ADF)

Dedication:

To the people in Muin Mound Grove, ADF
And ADF as a whole,
Who can't seem to get enough about the oghams.

Ogham: The Secret Language of the Druids
By Rev. Robert Lee (Skip) Ellison
Published by Ár nDraíocht Féin Publishing
ISBN 0-9765681-1-X
Copyright © 2007 by Rev. Robert Lee (Skip) Ellison
All rights reserved.

This book may not be reproduced, in whole or in part,
In any format or medium whatsoever,
Without permission of the author.

Much of the material in this book was also printed in
The Druids Alphabet:
What Do We Know About the Oghams?
By Robert Lee (Skip) Ellison
Published in 2003 by Earth Religions Press,
A division of Dubsar House Publishing
ISBN 1-59405503-3
First Printing March 2002
Dragon's Keep Publishing, East Syracuse, NY
© 2002 by Robert Lee (Skip) Ellison

All manuscript photographs are
'By permission of the Royal Irish Academy © RIA'
The antiquity of the original documents accounts
for the quality of the reproduction.

Cover & book design by Sharon Smith
Cover Photograph by Medb Aodhamair

Table of Contents

Introduction:	A Short History of the Oghams	1
Chapter One:	Uses of the Oghams	3
Chapter Two:	The Tree Ogham	9
	First Aicme	13
	Second Aicme	23
	Third Aicme	33
	Fourth Aicme	43
	Fifth Aicme	53
	My Additions	59
Chapter Three:	Other Oghams from the Scholar's Primer	61
	The Forfeda Lists	63
	The Secret Writing Lists	66
	The Cipher Lists	76
	The Mnemonic Lists	92
	The Gesture Lists	95
	The Divination List	96
	The Numbering Lists	96
	The Tree Variant Lists	101
Chapter Four:	The Use of Oghams in Magic and Divination	103
	Oghams and Magic	103
	Why Do We Need to Know Divination?	105
	What Is Divination?	105
	How Are Divinations Done?	107
	General Guidelines for Divination Tools	110
	Ways to improve your Divination	110
	Ethics for the Diviner	111

Chapter Five:	The Battle of the Trees	113
	A Warning about Robert Graves	113
Appendix 1:	A Quick Refference - The Tree Ogham	125
Appendix 2:	Making Your Own Ogham Discs	129
Appendix 3:	Resources	141
Appendix 4:	Working with the Old Irish	145
Appendix 5:	A Word about Ár nDraíocht Féin	151

Introduction
A Short History of the Oghams

One of the most valuable sources for this book is *Auraicept na n-Éces: The Scholars' Primer*, edited by George Calder in 1917. It is subtitled, 'Being the texts of the ogham tract from the Book of Ballymote and the Yellow Book of Lecan', and the text of the *Trefhocul* from the Book of Leinster. My edition is the 1995 reprint.

The Primer (as I will refer to it) has the advantage of having the Irish on one page with the English translation on the facing page. Most scholars consider it one of the best texts available on the *Oghams* (in MI [Modern Irish], or *Ogam* in OI [Old Irish]). Other good texts on the Oghams are listed in Appendix 4.

It appears from looking at the ogham inscriptions in Ireland that the ogham alphabet originated around the time when the first ogham stones appeared. This would have placed its origin about the 4th century CE [Current Era, this is the preferred academic designation replacing AD]. This is about or a little after the time the Runic Alphabet appeared. Almost all of the surviving ogham inscriptions date from the 4th to the 8th centuries.

Although some scholars argue for an earlier date, as early as 6th – 3rd centuries BCE [Before Current Era][1], based on linguistic evidence. I feel that Dr. Simon James sums the debate on the age of the oghams up well in his book *"The World of the Celts"* where he says:

> "…Ogam (or Ogham) was a unique Irish writing, thought to have been inspired by contact with Latin writing, and especially Roman numerals. Made of simple strokes, it was easily cut on stone or wood, along a central line – usually the edge of a slab. Messages carved on wood are mentioned in the Tain, but the surviving texts are mostly names on tombstones (another imported Roman idea). Exactly when Ogam first appeared is still unclear, but sometime during the fourth century AD seems likely: Ogam stones were erected during the fifth to seventh centuries. They are found mainly in southern Ireland and western parts of Brit-

---

1 Griffen, Toby D. "On the Age of Ogham". *Celtic Studies Association of North America Journal.* 5/9-12/2002 issue. Page 7.

ain where the Irish settled. In Britain the Ogam text is often accompanied by a Latin version."[2]

Most scholars today believe that the surviving stone inscriptions are some form of markers, such as boundary markers, grave inscriptions, or memorial stones. Along with the inscriptions that translate into Irish, some appear to be Pictish oghams. While there are many academic "discussions" about these oghams, we really are not sure about their meanings.[3]

The Oghams are broken down into five groups, called *"aicme."* Each aicme (plural = *aicmi* = group or family), is composed of five further divisions. These divisions are each equal to an individual letter, called a "few" or *fid* (which actually means "tree" in Irish. If you have a group of letters, it is a *feda* in Irish. At times, you will see the vowels also referred to as the *feda*, with the consonants referred to as the *táebomnai* (side or bole of a tree in Irish). The first letter of the group, i.e. *Aicme Beithe* for the "B" group, and *Aicme hÚatha* for the "H" group, refers to the groups of ogham. One other term that you will see at times is *"druim"* which is the stemline and means ridge, or edge in Irish.[4]

The oghams on stones are read from the left side first, up the stone, then across the top (L-R) and down the right side. It is important to remember when going down the right side to shift your perspective, so that it is as if you are standing above the stone and looking down at it, which will then cause left and right to reverse. If there are inscriptions on both sides but none on the top, then they are read up both sides.

When written on a horizontal line, as in manuscripts, they are read from left to right. Many of the Oghams were designed to be used only in manuscripts and not on stones. Any that have curvy or wavy lines are meant for manuscripts. I will be talking more about them in Chapter 3.

---

[2] James, Simon. *The World of the Celts.* Thames and Hudson, London. 1993. ISBN – 0500050678. Page 163.
[3] For more information, see: A) Griffen, Toby D., The Grammar of the Pictish Symbol Stones. LACUS Forum 27 (2001), 217-26. http://www.geocities.com/~dubricius/lacus00.pdf; B) Forsyth, Katherine. Language in Pictland. http://eprints.gla.ac.uk/2081/ - accessed 2/26/07
[4] McManus, Damien. A Guide to Ogham. Leinster Leader Ltd., Kildare, Ireland. 1991. ISBN – 1870684753. Page 3.

Uses of the Oghams

Very often, you will read where modern authors talk about how the ogham was developed to 'teach us the secrets of the trees'. This is incorrect in many respects! First of all, the tree ogham is only ONE of 150 different types of ogham. Second, there are at least two other variations of the tree ogham, that some scholars feel represent different species of the same trees. And third, it is apparent from reading the original material, that the main reason the trees, or animals, or birds, or whatever were chosen, was because of the initial sound ONLY. Now, with that misconception out of the way, let's move on to the real uses of the oghams.

As far as historians can tell, there have been at least seven uses of the ogham. They are: as a normal alphabet, as secret writings, as codes, as a mnemonic list to memorize important information, as a gesture language, for divination and for magical purposes.

A.   Normal Alphabet

Starting first with the use as a normal alphabet, which is VERY likely the primary use of the oghams, there are two stories about how the oghams were developed. In the first, Fenius Farsaidh listened to all the other languages at the Tower of Nimrod and out of all of them developed a language that had all the best features. This language was Irish. After developing the language, he needed a way to write the language down, so the oghams were invented.[1]

We find the second version in *In Lebor Ogaim*, one of the principle ogham tracts that have come down to us from the Old Irish period. As Damian McManus quotes it in *"A Guide to Ogham,"* it reads:

> "The inventor here is Ogma mac Elathan who is said to have been skilled in speech and poetry and to have created the system as proof of his intellectual ability and with the intention that it should be the preserve of the learned, to the exclusion of the rustics and fools."[2]

---

[1] Calder, George (ed). *Auraicept Na N-Éces: The Scholars Primer*. Four Courts Press, Portland, OR. 1995. ISBN - 1851821813. Page 79.
[2] McManus, Damien. *A Guide to Ogham*. Leinster Leader Ltd., Kildare, Ireland. 1991. ISBN – 1870684753. Page 150.

The full text of this passage also includes the use of secret writing as the first message written in ogham, talked about below. Ogma is known from the tales as one of the Túatha Dé Danann who was skilled in strength and though of by some as the Irish Hercules.

We see another use of the oghams as an alphabet in the *"The Voyage of Bran Mac Febal."* In this story, Bran is said to have written down more than fifty quatrains of poetry in Ogham to tell of his voyages:

> "66. Thereupon, to the people of the gathering Bran told all his wanderings from the beginning until that time. And he wrote these quatrains in Ogham, and then bade them farewell. And from that hour his wanderings are not known."[3]

Last, in the *'Book of Leinster'*, there is a reference to a library, *tech screpta* in Old Irish, of "rods of the *Fili*" [poets] that were cut in Ogham on wood. This library was kept at Tara. Sad to say, all of it is now lost.

After the Greek language came to Ireland, they needed other symbols for the diphthongs, the extra sounds found in the new language, which they had brought with them, and so they added the *Forfeda* (plural, singular is *Forfid* – extra or additional letters). There are actually many groups of *Forfeda*, as you will see in the chapter on The Other Oghams.

B. Secret Writing Oghams

There are a few references in the tales of the ogham being used as a form of secret writing. In the first, supposed to be the first message written in ogham, a message was written on a birch rod consisting of seven individual strokes. This was the letter 'B' written seven times. This story is sometimes told with seven birch branches being used. This message was for Lugh and he interpreted it to mean that his wife would be carried off seven times into the Sidhe mounds unless she was protected by birch.[4]

Another tale, found in the *Táin Bó Cuailnge*, the Cattle Raid of Cooley, tells of Cúchulainn, an Irish hero, leaving a hoop formed from an oak sapling on top of a standing stone as a warning for the army of Connacht. On the hoop he had carved letters in ogham. None of the army could understand the meaning until Fergus mac Róich found it. Fergus, who was a Druid with the army, interpreted it to mean that the army could not pass unless there

---

3 From - http://www.maryjones.us/ctexts/branvoyage.html - accessed 2/26/07.
4 Calder, George (ed). *Auraicept Na N-Éces: The Scholars Primer*. Four Courts Press, Portland, OR. 1995. ISBN - 1851821813. Page 91.

Chapter 1 - Uses of the Oghams

was someone with the army that could duplicate Cúchulainn's feats, other than Fergus.

Within the Primer, there are 43 types of oghams used for secret writing. I will be describing these oghams in further detail in Chapter 4.

C. Cipher or Code Oghams

There are three of the "other oghams" that are specifically referred to as "cipher oghams," oghams used to hide the meaning of the message. They are 1) Head in Bush or Persisting Ogham (#25) – these numbers refer to the numbering system used in Chapter 3). 2) Head Under Bush Ogham (#26) and 3) Serpent About Head Ogham (#27). Along with these oghams, specifically called "cipher oghams," another 38 oghams are used as ciphers in that the order of the letters is changed in different ways.

I differentiate between cipher oghams and secret writing oghams by the way the letters are formed. If they are using normal fews but changing the order of the letters or adding in extra letters, then I consider it a cipher ogham. If they are using different marks for the fews, then I consider it a secret writing ogham. These oghams will be described in further detail in Chapter 4 on the other oghams.

D. Mnemonic Lists To Memorize Important Information

Included in the "other oghams" are eleven types of oghams where the names of important things or people were used for each letter. For example, in the River Pool Ogham (#2) each letter is symbolized by the name of a famous river pool – B = Barrow & L = Lower Shannon, etc. In the Bird Ogham (#4) each letter is symbolized by a type of bird – B = *besan* (pheasant) & L = *lachu* (duck), etc.

E. Gesture Language

Ogham was used as a gesture language as well. By this, I mean that it was a sign language, rather than a spoken language. Some of the oghams used in this manner are 1) Foot Ogham (#18), 2) Nose Ogham (#19) 3) Palm of Hand Ogham (#20), and 4) Shin Ogham (which is not listed with those in the Primer but is referred to by McManus in several writings). In these oghams, the body part in the name was used as the stem line, the line against which the ogham was formed.

F. Divination

Many people use the ogham today as a tool for divination, although there are not too many examples of it from the ancient literature. We do have one of the "other oghams," the Boy Ogham (#17), which is specifically used for divining the sex of an unborn child. In this ogham, the pregnant woman's' name is divided into individual letters and the letters are counted. If she bore a child previously, it is the previous child's' name which is divided and counted. If there is a letter over, i.e. the name has an odd number of letters; then the child will be a boy. If the name has an even number of letters, the child will be a girl.

McManus describes another instance of divination using the oghams that comes from *Tochmarc Étáine*, 'The Wooing of Etaine' (quoting Windisch, 1880 [Irische Texte mit Wörterbuch], 129, § 18). He gives the quote as:

> "After Midir's abduction of Etain, Eochaid sends forth his messengers to search for her and he himself seeks her out for a year and a day, but to no avail. He then gives his druid Dallan the task of finding her. Dallan is troubled by her disappearance for over a year and 'he makes four rods of yew and writes Ogam (*oghumm*) in them and it is revealed to him through his keys of science (*triana eochraib ecsi*) and through his Ogam (*ocus triana oghumm*)' that Etain is in the sid of Bri Leith, having been carried there by Midir."[5]

My only problem with this is that I cannot find this reference in either of the two English translations of this story that I know of online. With the first located at: http://www.maryjones.us/ctexts/etain.html and the next at the CELT site located at: http://www.ucc.ie/celt/published/T301021/index.html and even more importantly, I cannot find it in the Old Irish version that is located at the CELT site at: http://www.ucc.ie/celt/published/G301900/text035.html. This quote is frequently found in online sources but until I can read it in the original, I have to consider it very suspicious.

It would be nice if I could find proof for this method, because it does sound very similar to the reference in the *Agricola* and the *Germania*, by Tacitus, about the tribes of Germany using fl at rods of nut-bearing wood to divine. He may have been referring to ogham rods instead of, or as well as, rune staves.

---

5 McManus, Damien. *A Guide to Ogham*. Leinster Leader Ltd., Kildare, Ireland. 1991. ISBN – 1870684753 Page 157.

There is one other method of divination using oghams, the *crannchur*, that I have seen referenced online, but have not been able to prove by reading about it in any of the Old Irish manuscripts. A description of it from the Celtic Planet website reads:

> "Ogham is often used for divination in mythology as well as pseudo-history. In the *Seanchus Mór* (The Irish Law Tracts), a method of divining the guilt of a suspected criminal is described. The *crannchur*, 'casting of the woods,' used three marked lots representing innocence, guilt, and the Trinity. They are drawn and replaced until either the innocent or guilty lot is taken. The text does not say how the lots were marked, but Ogham is a strong possibility as it was used elsewhere such as on the bone and wooden dice/lots found at Ballinderry, Co. Offaly."[6]

Crannchur in Old Irish does mean lots or casting lots, so this may be an authentic method, and I just haven't found the correct references.

In this book, I'll be giving some of the meanings that can be used for divination, taken from the Primer as well as some associations for the different trees. The meanings from the Primer are called 'kennings' for the trees and were used in the poetic language of the Bards to add layers of meanings to their poetry. In Chapter 4 on divination, I will be going into more detail on how the Oghams can be used for this purpose.

G. Magical Purposes

There have been a few items found with both ogham writing and other symbols on them that have been interpreted as being used for a magical purpose. In the following picture[7], you can see the special markings on the sheep bone.*(see next page)* Because these do not translate completely using any of the ogham scripts, it is assumed they were used for a magical purpose as a talisman or perhaps for divination.

Another talisman used for healing purposes is an amber bead inscribed with the word *atucmlu* in OI. The meaning of this word is unknown. The use of the bead that has came down in the O'Connor family, which has always owned it, is as a cure for eye problems and as an aid in childbirth. It is now in the British Museum.

---

6 Lavelle, Brian. "An Overview of the Ogham Script". From http://www.thecelticplanet.com/ogham.htm - accessed 2/26/07
7 Macalister, R.A.S. *Corpus Inscriptionum Insularum Celticarum*. Four Courts Press, Dublin, Ireland. 1996 edition. ISBN- 1851822429. Pages 56 & 57.

Ogham: The Secret Language of the Druids

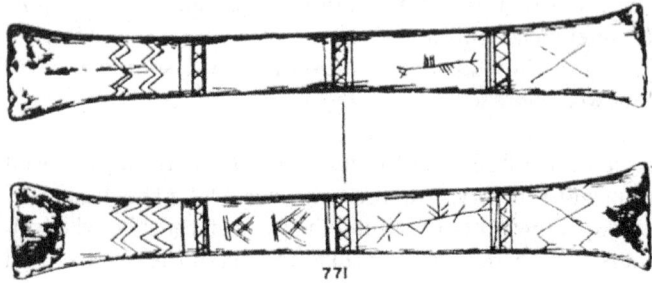

A large slab of rock, found in the excavation of an old stone hut on the southern slope of Mount Eagle in County Kerry, bears markings that cannot be interpreted by normal means. These markings bear a slight resemblance to the ones on the amber bead and the slab may have been used for healing purposes, but no actual history of the use of the slab is known. I will go into further detail on these objects and other aspects of the use of the Oghams in magic in Chapter 4.

2

The Tree Ogham

The Tree Ogham is the best known of all the Oghams and as I stated in the beginning of Chapter 1, is what most people think of as the only Ogham.

I am going to begin this chapter with a statement that many readers will find astonishing, if not outright false. That is that most academics today believe that the original use of tree ogham was not to describe the trees of the forest, nor was it based on the characteristics of the trees. Medieval copyist who did not understand what they were copying started that idea, called an "alphabet vegetal" by McManus. As he says in *Irish Letter Names and Their Kennings*,

> "It has become a commonplace of Irish scholarship to regard all the Irish letter-names as names of trees and no other aspect of Irish letters has contributed more to the derailment of a serious study of the history of Ogam than this."[1]

There are two very good articles in the academic journals that discuss the real meanings for the names of the oghams. The first, by Howard Meroney and titled *"Early Irish Letter-Names,"* was published in the magazine *Speculum* (Vol. 24, No. 1. (January 1949), pages 19-43.)[2] I feel that this is one of the best articles there is discussing the real meaning of the ogham names and letters. I will be referring to it, and the article below, throughout the chapter on the Tree Oghams.

The second article is the one referred to earlier by Damian McManus, published in *Ériu* magazine in 1988. This magazine is not available through JSTOR, but is available through the Royal Irish Academy website.[3] This in-depth article goes along with the Meroney article, and they both show the origins of the letters. Both articles are must-have articles for the serious ogham researcher.

There are at least two different opinions about the layout of the Tree Oghams, whether it was *Beithe* (pronounced 'beh') – *Luis* (pr. 'lweesh') – *Nion* (pr. 'ne-un') or *Beithe* – *Luis* – *Fern* (pr. 'fair-n'); usually referred to as

---

1 McManus, Damien. *Irish Letter Names and Their Kennings*. Ériu, XXXIX (1988). Page 129.
2 This article is available through the JSTOR article archive at: http:/links.jstor.org/sici?sici=0038-7134%28194901%2924%3A1%3C19%3AEIL%3E2.0.CO%3B2-0.
3 http://shop.ria.ie/shop/shopdisplayproducts.asp?id=19&cat=%C9RIU – accessed 2/26/07.

9

BLN or BLF. Based on my studies, I believe that the correct layout is BLF and that is the order that I use.

Another difference of opinion arises over the use of the fifth aicme. Again, these are known by the name of *Forfeda* and are not part of the original set of twenty trees that were used. It is thought that they represent the Greek diphthongs, and were added after the original group of four aicmes was developed.

There are actually four sets of *Forfeda* and we can find instances where the set listed here was included on some of the Ogham stones still in existence. I feel that at least this first set of *Forfeda* was used for writing and probably for divination and magical purposes as well.

In the magical training system, I have developed, I have added in three trees to the Oghams to be used as modifiers. I will be talking more about the trees I have chosen and reasons why in the section on other symbols.

An easy way to remember the order of the Tree Ogham is taken from the Primer, on pages 71-73:

> "These are their signs: right of stem, left of stem, athwart of stem, through stem, about stem. Thus is a tree climbed, to wit, treading on the root of the tree with thy right hand first and thy left hand after. Then with the stem, and against it, and through it and about it."

For the aicme and fews below, I will give the kennings from the four 'schools' of Ogham. The first is from the Word Ogham of Morann Mac Main and can be found on pages 277-285 in the Primer. The second is from the Word Ogham of Mac ind Óic and can be found on pages 285-289 in the Primer. The third is from the school of Fenius Farsaidh and can be found on pages 275-277 in the Primer. The fourth is from the Word Ogham of Cúchulainn, *Briatharogam Con Culainn*, found in Damian McManus' book, *A Guide to Ogham* on pages 42 & 43.

One other early tale has a bit of tree lore hidden in it, and that is "*Buile Suibhne* (The Frenzy of Suibhne) being The Adventures of *Suibhne Geilt.*"[4] While it does not talk about all the trees, it does refer to some of them. To summarize the tale, a king goes mad and lives for a year in the forests, spending each night perched in a tree. At the end of the year, he talks about the trees and tells of their virtues. I will be referring to the tale here as "Mad

---

4 From http://www.ucc.ie/celt/published/T302018/index.html - accessed 2/28/07.

Sweeney." Lastly, the sixth is my interpretations of the meanings for the Oghams.

The first seven associations are based on the "Other Oghams" that I will be talking about in Chapter 3. There have been many lists of associations developed and I cannot honestly agree with all of them. Ogham, as it was developed, is a system based on sound, especially the sound of the initial letter of the word. If the name of the object associated with the tree does not begin with the same letter in Old Irish or even in Modern Irish, then the association is a modern one not based on the letter sound and could not be right according to the old system.

Now if you wanted to add more associations with each one, all you would have to do is find the corresponding word in Old Irish (or Modern Irish if there is no word extant in Old Irish) for the class you are looking for. For example, if you wanted to add associations with animals, you would find the animal whose name began with the same letter as the tree. This is what I have done in the last three associations—Animal, Herb and Stone. Then, I finish the section on each tree by describing some ways it has been used in magic.

Each of the Ogham letters in the following discussion is shown as if carved on a wooden tile and oriented horizontally. Oghams were also carved vertically, rotated 90° clockwise. Thus the first one, Beith, can be seen on ancient stones as either ⊤ or ⊢.

Chapter 2 - The Tree Ogham

First Aicme

First Aicme- First Few

The standard name for this symbol is *Beith*, pronounced 'beh.' It has also been written as *Beth*[1], *Beith*[2] and *Beith*[3]. In English, it represents the letter B. The tree associated with this symbol is the European Birch, *Betula pendula*. This is one of the Peasant trees. By "Peasant Tree', I am referring to a list in the Brehon Laws that divides the trees of the forest into four classes based on their economic worth. They are herb trees, shrub trees, peasant trees and chieftain trees.[4] It is from this listing that I choose the trees for my magical training system.

Kennings:

Morann Mac Main – "faded trunk and fair hair."
Mac ind Óic – "most silvery of skin."
Fenius Farsaidh – "of withered trunk fair-haired the birch."
Cúchulainn – "beauty of the eyebrow."
Mad Sweeney – "o birch, smooth and blessed, thou melodious, proud one, delightful each entwining branch in the top of thy crown."
Ellison – new beginnings.

Notes on the name

Both Meroney and McManus feel that this letter-name does actually refer to the Birch tree based on the kennings.

Associated with: English (*Irish*)

Bird – Pheasant (*Besan*) (Taken from the Bird Ogham #4)
River Pool – (*Barrow*) (Taken from the River Pool Ogham #2)
Fortress (*Bruden*) (Taken from the Fortress Ogham #3)
Color – White (*Bán*) (Taken from the Color Ogham #5)
Agricultural – Axe (*Biail*) (Taken from the Agricultural Ogham #9)
Art – Livelihood (*Bethumnacht*) (Taken from the Art Ogham #22)
Saint – Brenainn (Taken from the Saint Ogham #21)

---

1 As used by Robert Graves in *The White Goddess* and by Nigel Pennick in *The Celtic Oracle*.
2 As used by Edred Thorsson, AKA Stephen Flowers.
3 As used by Michael Everson.
4 Kelly, Fergus. *A Guide to Early Irish Law*. Dublin Institute for Advanced Studies – Dublin. ISBN – 0901282952. Page 380.

Animal – Cow (*Bó*) (Created by myself based on the other Oghams)
Herb – Kale (*Braisech*) (Except for this first one, created by myself)
Stone – Beryl (*Beiril*) (Created by myself based on the other Oghams)

Magic and the Tree

Along with being a pioneer, this tree is also known as a mother tree, a fact acknowledged by the American Forestry Association who chose this tree as the First Mother Tree of America in 1920. In Brittany, the leaves from the Birch were placed in cradles to strengthen newborns; and in some places, the wood from the tree was used to make cradles for the same reason. Among the Norse, the birch represents the Earth Mother and is noted for its healing powers, growth, and the natural world.

In Russia, this tree was the symbol of health and the spirits of the forest. The *Lieschi*, forest spirits, lived in the tops of the trees and to invoke them, you had to cut branches from a young tree. You then placed the branches in a circle with the stems facing inward and stepped into the circle formed. By facing east and then bending your head down to looks between your legs, you could call them. In Russia, it was also believed that by tying a red ribbon around a birch tree, you would protect it from storms.

First Aicme - Second Few

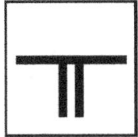
The standard name for this symbol is *Luis*, pronounced 'lweesh'. In English, it represents the letter L. The tree associated with this symbol is the European Mountain Ash, also known as the Rowan tree or the Quicken tree, *Sorbus aucuparia*. This is one of the Peasant trees.

Kennings:

Morann Mac Main – "delight of eye."
Mac ind Óic – "friend of cattle, dear to the cattle is elm for its bloom and for down."
Fenius Farsaidh – "delight of eye owing to the beauty of its berries."
Cúchulainn – "sustenance of cattle."
Mad Sweeney – "o quicken, little berried one, delightful is thy bloom."
Ellison - protection and control of the senses.

Notes on the name

This is the first of the letter-names that both Meroney and McManus feel do not belong to a tree. They both feel that this letter-name originally had the meaning of flame, or blaze, or radiance.

Associated with: English (*Irish*)

Bird – Duck (*Lachu*)
River Pool – Lower Shannon
Fortress – (*Liffy*)
Color – Grey (*Liath*)
Agriculture – Rope (*Loman*)
Art – Pilotage (*Luamnacht*)
Saint – Laisren
Animal – Frog (*Loscann*)
Herb – Mugwort (*Liathlus*)
Stone – Lead (*Luaidhe*)

Magic and the Tree

Rowan is a tree of protection and magic. This is one of the three trees, along with yew and ash, which Druid wands were made of and is helpful is shape changing spells. Rowan wood is very good to use for dowsing water.

Rowan staffs are said to protect the hiker from harm on journeys. Sailors would carry rowan wood or dried berries with them on voyages to protect themselves from storms at sea. It is thought that the five pointed star, or pentagram on the bottom of the berries was the source for the protection. In Scotland, rowan trees were planted on graves to prevent the dead from wandering again. They are also planted near houses there to protect from lightning. Small rowan crosses are sown into clothes while singing a protective charm to keep the wearers safe.

In Ireland, people tell that the rowan tree was brought into Ireland by the *Túatha Dé Danann*, and that it always retained its connection with the faeries.

We can use rowan in our magic whenever we need to work with the faeries or in spells involving protection or shape changing.

Chapter 2 - The Tree Ogham

First Aicme – Third Few

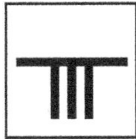

The standard name for this symbol is *Fern*, pronounced 'fairn'. In English, it represents the letter F or more often V. The tree associated with this symbol is the European Alder, *Alnus glutinosa*. This is one of the Peasant trees.

Kennings:

Morann Mac Main – "shield of warrior-bands owing to their redness or because the alder is the material of the shield."
Mac ind Óic – "guarding of milk for it is it that guards the milk, for of it are made the vessels containing the milk."
Fenius Farsaidh – "the van of the Warrior-bands for therefore are the shields."
Cúchulainn – "protection of the heart."
Mad Sweeney – "o alder, thou art not hostile, delightful is thy hue, thou art not rending and prickling in the gap wherein thou art."
Ellison – guidance, through its association with Bran the Blessed.

Notes on the name

Both Meroney and McManus agree that the kennings do point to the tree, although mainly from the use of the wood, not the shape or description of the tree.

Associated with: English (*Irish*)

Bird – Gull (*Fælinn*)
River Pool – (*Foyle*)
Fortress – (*Femen*)
Color – Red (*Flann*)
Agriculture – Hedge-bill (*Fidba*)
Art – Poetry (*Filideacht*)
Saint – Finnen
Animal – Mare (*Fàlaire*)
Herb – Seaweed (*Feamainn*)
Stone – Bronze (*Fionndruinne*)

Magic and the Tree

In the tale, "Battle of the Trees," the alder was the Battle Witch of all woods. It was found in the front line of battle and was vanquished by the ash tree.

Another reference to this tree is in one of the riddles of Taliesin, where he asks, "Why is the alder purple?" The answer is "Because Bran wore purple."

This comes from the fact that the supports of the Tower of London, where Bran's head lies, were made of alder wood and that the alder "bleeds" purple when cut. For magical purposes, we use alder in oracular spells, from its associations with Bran, and in protection spells, from its association as the Battle Witch.

First Aicme – Fourth Few

The standard name for this symbol is *Sail*, pronounced 'sahl'. It is also written as *Saille*[1]. In English, it represents the letter S. The tree associated with this symbol is the Osier Willow, *Salix viminalis*. This is one of the Peasant trees.

Kennings:

Morann Mac Main – "hue of the lifeless, i.e., hue of one dead, for denial, so that he is not living but dead."
Mac ind Óic – "activity of bees, for its bloom and for its catkin."
Fenius Farsaidh – "the color of a lifeless one, i.e., it has no color, owing to the resemblance of its hue to a dead person."
Cúchulainn – "beginning of honey."
Mad Sweeney – Not given.
Ellison - mysteries and water related subjects, also feminine attributes.

Notes on the name

This is another of the trees where Meroney and McManus agree the kennings refer to the tree.

Associated with: English (*Irish*)

Bird – Hawk (*Seg*)
River Pool – Shannon
Fortress – (*Seolae*)
Color - Fine-colored (*Sodath*)
Agriculture – Packsaddle (*Srathar*)
Art – Handicraft (*Sairsi*)
Saint – Sincheall
Animal – Fox (*Sionnach*)
Herb – Primrose (*Sabhaircin*)
Stone – Cat's Eye (*Suíl Cat*)

Magic and the Tree

The willow tree has long been associated with changes, probably from its ability to bend and sway. Legend says that the sisters of Phaeton, who were weeping at his death, changed into willows and that the flow of their tears, are the cause of the cascade of leaves found in the weeping willow.

---

1 As used by Robert Graves in *The White Goddess* and by Nigel Pennick in *The Celtic Oracle.*

In some of the European countries, willows are avoided after dark because it is said that they walk and will follow travelers. They have long been associated with magic dealing with the moon, and with water; probably because they are one of the trees that like to "keep their feet wet." Because willow trees usually grow near sacred wells, they are one of the trees that people tie "wish cloths" or "clooties" to in Ireland.

We can use willow in our magic for spells that deal with changes or that use the elemental power of water in them.

First Aicme – Fifth Few

The standard name for this symbol is *Nion*, pronounced 'ne-un'. It is also written as *Nin*[1] and *Nuin*[2]. In English, it represents the letter N. The tree associated with this symbol is the Ash, *Fraxinus excelsior*. This is one of the Chieftain trees.

Kennings:

Morann Mac Main – "checking of peace: it is the maw of a weaver's beam as applied to wood: a sign of peace is that."
Mac ind Óic – "fight of women, of the weaver's beam, i.e., maw of weaver's beam."
Fenius Farsaidh – "a check on peace is ash, for of it are made the spear-shafts by which the peace is broken: or that is a maw of a weaver's beam which is made of ash, that is, in time of peace weaver's beams are raised."
Cúchulainn – "boast of beauty."
Mad Sweeney – "o ash-tree, thou baleful one, hand-weapon of a warrior."
Ellison – ancient knowledge and the weaver's beam.

Notes on the name

The meaning of this letter name is one of the hardest for both Meroney and McManus. As McManus says in his article, "The kennings on this lettername and the name itself present a number of difficulties which I cannot solve."[3] In the end, he feels that its original meaning is "letter," and that the kennings were derived from alternative meanings that were not often used, such as "fork," as in a forked stick. In later times, the initial "N or nin," used as an abbreviation in the manuscripts, was an all-purpose initial that could designate any letter.

Associated with: English (*Irish*)

Bird – Snipe (*Næscu*)
River Pool – (*Nith*)
Fortress – (*Nephin*)
Color – Clear (*Necht*)
Agriculture – Ring (*Nasc*)
Art – Notary Work (*Notaireacht*)
Saint – Neasan

---

1 As used by Edred Thorsson – AKA Stephen Flowers.
2 As used by Michael Everson.
3 McManus, Damien. "Irish Letter Names and Their Kennings". *Ériu*, XXXIX (1988). Page 131.

Animal – Adder (*Nathair*)
Herb – Stinging Nettle (*Neantóg*)
Stone – Serpentine (*Nathartha*)

Magic and the Tree

For the Norse, the ash is both the world tree, Yggdrasil and the tree used to make the first man, Aska. Among the Celtic tribes, it was considered a tree of luck, maybe through its connections with battles. It was used for spear and arrow shafts and it is said that even Cupid's arrows are made from ash wood. Ash is also one of the favorite woods to use as a Maypole or in ritual fires.

Three of the five great trees of Ireland are ash, the Tree of Tortu, the Bough of Dathi and the Ash of Uisnech. It is said that they were cut down in 665CE as a sign of Christianity's triumph in Ireland.

Also in Ireland, we find several references to ash being used for healing purposes. It is told that in several places, ash trees were split while young and as they grew large, children would be passed through the split to heal them. There is an old charm about using pins that had first been stuck in an ash tree to heal warts. It reads, "ashen tree, ashen tree, pray buy these warts off of me."[4]

In our magic, we can use ash any time we need strength or courage. It can also be used in protection, healing, or creation spells or as a symbol of male energy.

---

[4] Hopman, Ellen Evert. *Tree Medicine, Tree Magic*. Phoenix Publishing Inc., Custer, WA. 1991. ISBN – 0-919345-55-7. Page 40.

Second Aicme

Second Aicme – First Few

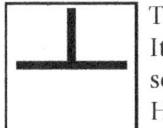 The standard name for this symbol is *Uath*, pronounced 'ooah'. It is also written as *Huath*[1] and *hÚath*[2]. In English, it represents the letter H. The tree associated with this symbol is the Hawthorn, also known as Whitethorn due to its blossoms, or *Crataegus monogyna*. This is one of the Peasant trees.

Kennings:

Morann Mac Main – "pack of wolves, for a terror to any one is a pack of wolves, owing to the affinity of the name, for they are a thorn, in the same way."
Mac ind Óic – "blanching of face, for blanched is a man's face when he is encompassed with fear or terror."
Fenius Farsaidh – "because it is formidable owing to its thorns."
Cúchulainn – "most difficult at night."
Mad Sweeney – while not in the main section that tells of the trees, there is one verse about the hawthorn –

> "...he happened one night to be on the top of a tall ivy-clad hawthorn tree which was in the glen. It was hard for him to endure that bed, for at every twist and turn he would give, a shower of thorns off the hawthorn would stick in him, so that they were piercing and rending his side and wounding his skin."

Ellison - counseling, protection and cleansing.

Notes on the name

Both Meroney and McManus agree that this letter-name means "fear or horror" and has nothing at all to do with the whitethorn tree. McManus feels that the association with whitethorn appears to have come from the early copyists attempt to reconcile "fear" with the "pack of hounds" kenning.

Meroney feels that the association comes from the idea that the symbol set upright, with the line pointing up, resembles a "thorn." McManus refutes this idea in his article.

---

1 As used by Nigel Pennick in the Celtic Oracle and by Edred Thorsson – AKA Stephen Flowers.
2 As used by Michael Everson and McManus.

Associated with: English (*Irish*)

Bird – Night Raven (*Hadaig*)
River Pool – (*Othain Fahan*)
Fortress – (*hOcha*)
Color – Terrible (*Huath*)
Agriculture – ?[indicates that translation is unknown] (*Huartan*)
Art – Trisyllacic Poetry (*Airchetul*)
Saint – Adamnan
Animal – Piglet (*Arcán*)
Herb – Yarrow (*Athair*)
Stone – Silver (*Airgead*)

Magic and the Tree

This tree, known as one of the trees of the Faeries, is a powerful tree to use in any magic involving them. One story involving the tree is that while they were building the DeLorean car factory Northern Ireland, they took down a lone hawthorn tree. A single hawthorn is known in Ireland as an entrance into a faerie mound. None of the workers wanted to remove it, so DeLorean himself, climbed on the machine and took it out. Removing this tree angered the Faeries, and that is why the business collapsed.

In Greece, brides would carry the hawthorn blossoms on their wedding day as the tree was favored by Hymen.

We can use this in our magic in several ways. It can be used in purification, protection, cleansing, fertility and marital happiness spells. The tree itself can be used as a wishing tree by tying bits of cloth on it.

Second Aicme – Second Few

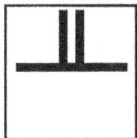 The standard name for this symbol is *Dair*, pronounced 'dah-r'. It is also written as *Duir*[1]. In English, it represents the letter D. The tree associated with this symbol is the English Oak, *Quercus robur*. This is one of the Chieftain trees.

Kennings:

Morann Mac Main – "highest of bushes, with respect to its wood in the forest."
Mac ind Óic – "carpenter's work."
Fenius Farsaidh – "higher than bushes is an oak."
Cúchulainn – "most carved of craftsmanship."
Mad Sweeney – "thou oak, bushy, leafy, thou art high beyond trees…" and later – "my aversion in woods - I conceal it not from anyone - is the leafy stirk of an oak swaying evermore. (?)" [The question mark is by the translator and I am not sure what he means by this either.]
Ellison - wisdom and strength.

Notes on the name

This is another name where both Meroney and McManus feel it refers to the tree.

Associated with: English (*Irish*)

Bird – Wren (*Droen*)
River Pool – (*Dergderg*)
Fortress – (*Dinn Ríg*)
Color – Black (*Dub*)
Agricultural – Cask (*Dabach*)
Art – Wizardry (*Druidheacht*)
Saint – Donnan
Animal – Ox (*Damh*)
Herb – Mistletoe (*Drualus*)
Stone – Diamond (*Diamant*)

Magic and the Tree

Oaks are one of the trees of the Druids and many think that the term Druid

---

1 As used by Robert Graves in *The White Goddess*, Nigel Pennick in *The Celtic Oracle* and by Edred Thorsson – AKA Stephen Flowers.

itself derives from this association. We have a reference from Pliny to the Druids harvesting mistletoe from it on the 6th day of the moon. Hollow trees in English folklore are seen as an entrance to the faerie worlds. It was suppose to be in one of these hollow trees that Merlin was imprisoned.

Among the Romans and Greeks, oak was given as a nuptial gift as a sign of fertility. It was also known as an oracular tree and both Jupiter and Athena spoke through it.

The fruit of the oak, the acorn, has several magic uses. It has been set in windows to protect the house from lightning and carried to prevent illness or pain. It can also be planted in the dark of the moon to bring about financial success. They can also be carried as symbols of immortality and longevity.

We can use the oak in our magic whenever strength or nobility is needed. It can be used as a symbol of a gateway or entrance into the land of Faerie. Acorns can be used in spells as symbols of male energy, symbols of immortality or a food for the faeries.

Chapter 2 - The Tree Ogham

Second Aicme – Third Few

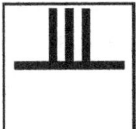

The standard name for this symbol is *Tinne*, pronounced 'chinyuh'. In English, it represents the letter T. The tree associated with this symbol is the Holly, *Ilex aquifolium*. This is one of the Chieftain trees.

Kennings:

Morann Mac Main – "another thing the meaning of that today."
Mac ind Óic – "fires of coal."
Fenius Farsaidh – "a third of a wheel is holly, because holly is one of the three timbers of the chariot-wheel."
Cúchulainn – "one of three parts of a weapon."
Mad Sweeney – "o holly, little sheltering one, thou door against the wind…"
Ellison – justice and balance.

Notes on the name

Both Meroney and McManus agree that the original meaning of this letter-name is "bar of metal." A recent discovery in the UK identified the wood in a chariot wheel as holly, so the kennings may be factual.

Associated with: English (*Irish*)

Bird – Starling (*Truith*)
River Pool – (*Teith*)
Fortress – Tara
Color – Dark Grey (*Temen*)
Agriculture – Adze (*Tal*)
Art – Turning (*Tornoracht*)
Saint – (*Tighearnach*)
Animal – Boar (*Torc*)
Herb – Hound's Tounge (*Teanga Cú*)
Stone – Topaz (*Tópáz*)

Magic and the Tree

Holly is another plant with a long history of magical uses. In England in medieval times, people placed it around the beds of young girls to "prevent them from turning into witches." There is an old saying that if you pick nine holly leaves and tie them with nines knots in a three-cornered handkerchief and place them under your pillow, you will dream of your future love or cause your dream to come true.

It was often planted near houses to protect them from lightning and as a general protective herb. It was said that if green holly leaves were burned, there would be a death in the family.

Holly is one of the plants tied to the seasons. It was only to be brought into the house near Christmas and had to be out by the end of Twelfth Night or there would be one accident for each leaf in the house.

In our magic, we can use holly in seasonal spells, protection spells or oracular spells. It is also very good to use in ritual or magical fires.

Second Aicme – Fourth Few

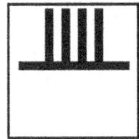

The standard name for this symbol is *Coll*, pronounced 'cull'. In English, it represents the letter C. The tree associated with this symbol is the Hazel, *Corylus avellana*. This is one of the Chieftain trees.

Kennings:

Morann Mac Main – "fairest of trees, owing to its beauty in woods."
Mac ind Óic – "friend of cracking." I believe that this refers to word cracking, a favorite pastime of the Druids.
Fenius Farsaidh – "fair wood, that is, every one is eating of its nuts."
Cúchulainn – "sweetest tree."
Mad Sweeney – "o hazlet, little branching one, o fragrance of hazel-nuts."
Ellison - wisdom and intuition.

Notes on the name

Both Meroney and McManus agree that letter-name refers to the hazel tree.

Associated with: English (*Irish*)

Bird – Crane (*Corr Mhóna*)[1]
River Pool – (*Catt*)
Fortress – (*Cera*)
Color – Brown (*Cron*)
Agriculture – Wagon (*Carr*)
Art – Harping (*Cruitireacht*)
Saint – Cronan
Animal – Hound (*Cú*)
Herb – Columbine (*Colaimbin*)
Stone – Copper (*Copar*)

Magic and the Tree

The hazel has been referred to in so many tales of magic that an entire workshop would be needed to list them all. It is one of the trees used to make wands, and in that form, it is used in shape shifting spells. It has also been used in spells for good luck and for protection from lightning and storms. It is said that medieval pilgrims protected themselves from hazards on the road by tying hazel branches on their staffs.

---

1 As used by Bill Elston.

Hazel is associated with knowledge and is the source of the nine hazels of wisdom whose nuts dropped into the well of Segais, the source of the River Boyne. They also grew over Connla's Well and dropped into it to produce the bubbles of inspiration. The salmon swimming in this well were filled with the bubble and eating them made you wise. It was one of these salmon that Fionn was cooking when he burned his thumb and stuck it in his mouth, giving him a 'Thumb of Knowledge or Inspiration.'

In Wales, hazel twigs were woven into wishing caps that would grant the desires of the wearers. For the Romans, Mercury's rod was made of hazel wood and was the symbol of communication and commerce. In some Roman weddings, hazel torches were burnt to produce peaceful and happy relationships.

In our magic, we can use hazel for spells dealing with wisdom, fertility, happiness or protection.

Second Aicme – Fifth Few

 The standard name for this symbol is *Ceirt*, pronounced 'kwurt'. It is also written as *Quert*[1] , *Queirt*[2] and *Cert*[3]. In English, it represents the letter Q. The tree associated with this symbol is the Crab Apple - *Malus sylvestris*. This is one of the Chieftain trees.

Kennings:

Morann Mac Main – "shelter of a hind, i.e., a fold: lunatic, that is death sense, it is then his sense comes to him when he goes to his death."
Mac ind Óic – "force of the man."
Fenius Farsaidh – "shelter of a wild hind."
Cúchulainn – "dregs of clothing."
Mad Sweeney – "o apple-tree, little apple-tree, much art thou shaken…"
Ellison – the Otherworld and choice.

Notes on the name

This letter-name means "rag," and both Meroney and McManus agree that it has nothing to do with the apple tree, which would have been aball in OI.

Associated with: English (*Irish*)

Bird – Hen (*Querc*)
River Pool – (*Cusrat*)
Fortress – (*Corann*)
Color – Mouse colored (*Quiar*)
Agriculture – Faggot (*Cual*)
Art – Fluting (*Quislenacht*)
Saint – Ciaran
Animal – Cricket (*Criogar*)
Herb – Cinquefoil (*Cuiqbhileach*)
Stone – Bloodstone (*Cloch Fhola*)

Magic and the Tree

The apple is associated with the Land of the Ever Young, the land of the faeries, and immortality. There are several references in the tales to 'Apple Branches,' made from gold with silver bells on them that would produce

---
1 As used by Robert Graves in *The White Goddess* and by Nigel Pennick in *The Celtic Oracle*.
2 As used by Edred Thorsson – AKA Stephen Flowers.
3 As used by Michael Everson.

happiness or sleep.

The apple tree was important to the people for the crops produced and each year at Yule, the people would go out Wassailing the trees, to wish them good growth and fertility for the coming year. The apple seeds were used in a form of divination to find a future husband or wife. The seeds were named and then thrown into a fire. The one that popped the loudest indicated the future mate.

Among the Romans, we find the tree that bore the golden apples that had been given to Hera as a wedding gift. These apples figured into the labors of Hercules and the only race that Atalanta lost, to her future husband Hippomenses.

Among the Norse, we find the golden apples of Iduna, the Lady of Youth. These apples were kept in a bottomless casket and the gods ate them daily to retain their youth. Apples were also sacred to Hel.

We can use apple wood and apples in love spells, fertility spells, divination, and spells relating to the faeries.

Third Aicme

Third Aicme – First Few

The standard name for this symbol is *Muin*, pronounced 'muhn'. In English, it represents the letter M. The tree associated with this symbol is the Vine, *Vitus* species. There are so many varieties in the British Isles, that it is impossible to narrow the species down any farther. This is one of the Herb trees.

Kennings:

Morann Mac Main – "strongest of effort, owing to the identity of name with muin, back of man or ox, for it is they that are the strongest in existence as regards effort."
Mac ind Óic – "condition of slaughter, to wit, a man's back."
Fenius Farsaidh – "highest of beauty is vine, that is because it grows aloft."
Cúchulainn – "path of the voices."
Mad Sweeney – While he does not talk about the vine, he does talk about the bramble, to which some people think this letter-name refers. For the bramble, he says, "o briar, little arched one, thou grantest no fair terms, thou ceasest not to tear me, till thou hast thy fill of blood."
Ellison – prophecy and inhibitions, or the lack of them.

Notes on the name

This letter-name has three meanings in OI. First, it means upper part of the back or neck. We see this in the first two kennings. The second meaning is ruse, trick, fate, or treachery. We see this in the second kennings, where the "trick" is the "condition of slaughter." In addition, the third meaning is love or esteem. We see this reflected in the third kenning. Looking at this, we see that the only connection seen with the vine is in the second kenning.

Associated with: English (*Irish*)

Bird – Titmouse (*Mintan*)
River Pool – (*Muinten*)
Fortress – (*Meath*)
Color – Variegated (*mBracht*)
Agriculture - ? (*Machad*)
Art – Soldiering (*Milaideacht*)
Saint – Manchan
Animal – Otter (*Madra Uisce*)

Herb – Mulberry (*Maoildearg*)
Stone – Malachite (*Malaicít*)

Magic and the Tree

Along with the magic of Dionysius with his wine, grape leaves have been used in healing spells. It is said that when they are wrapped around the head, hangovers will vanish. The vine is also very useful in magic acting as a binder, just as the vine can be woven into circles or tied together, so can the magic associated with it.

In our magics, we can use the vine as the wreath within which the magic resides or in magic requiring the loosening of inhibitions.

Third Aicme – Second Few

The standard name for this symbol is *Gort*, pronounced 'gort'. In English, it represents the letter G. The tree associated with this symbol is the English Ivy, *Hedera helix*. This is one of the Herb trees.

Kennings:

Morann Mac Main – "sweeter than grasses, owing to the identity of the name with the cornfield."
Mac ind Óic – "med nercc, to wit, ivy." Not really much to go on.
Fenius Farsaidh – "greener that pastures is ivy."
Cúchulainn – "sating of multitudes."
Mad Sweeney – "o ivy, little ivy, thou art familiar in the dusky wood."
Ellison – the search for yourself and inner wisdom.

Notes on the name

Both Meroney and McManus agree that the original meaning of this letter-name is "field."

Associated with: English (*Irish*)

Bird – Swan (*Géis*)
River Pool – (*Gavel*)
Fortress – (*Gabur*)
Color – Blue (*Gorm*)
Agriculture – Withe (*Gat*)
Art – Smithwork (*Gaibneacht*)
Saint – George
Animal – Goat (*Gabor*)
Herb – Chestnut (*Geanmchnù*)
Stone – Aquamarine (*Gormghlas*)

Magic and the Tree

Ivy, long used in garlands or crowns given to victors in contests in the Greek city-states, was also one of the favorite plants of Pan. There is a verse by the poet Drayton that talks about it. It reads: "To Pan we dedicate the Pine, whose slips the Shepard graceth; again the Ivy and the Vine on his swoln Bacchus placeth."[1]

---

[1] Friend, Hilderic. *Flower Lore*. Para research, Inc. Rockport, MA. 1981. ISBN 0-914918-32-X.

Because of its tenacity in holding on to walls, it has long been used in binding and friendship spells. In Victorian times, it was carried in the hands of mourners at funerals as a reminder of the soul's immortality.

We can use the Ivy in our magic in friendship and binding spells or in workings to Pan.

Third Aicme – Third Few

The standard name for this symbol is *nGéadal*, pronounced 'natal'. It is also written as *nGetal*[1]. In English, it represents the letters NG or GG. The tree associated with this symbol is the Broom, *Cytisus scoparius*. This is one of the Herb trees. Some other systems use the Reed for this symbol, but based on the Scholar's Primer, I use the Broom.

Kennings:

Morann Mac Main – "a physician's strength, because it is strength with the physicians, and there is an affinity between *cath*, panacea (?), and *getal*, broom."
Mac ind Óic – none given.
Fenius Farsaidh – "a physician's strength is broom."
Cúchulainn – "beginning of slaying."
Mad Sweeney – Not talked about.
Ellison – working and tools.

Notes on the name

Meroney feels that the original meaning of this letter-name is "charm." McManus refutes this, and argues for the meaning of "wounds." While both would fit the kennings, I think that McManus' argument is the more persuasive.

Associated with: English (*Irish*)

Bird – Goose (*nGéigh*)
River Pool – (*Graney*)
Fortress – (*nGarman*)
Color – Green (*nGlas*)
Agriculture – Wedge (*nGend*)
Art – Modeling (*nGibæ*)
Saint – (*nGeminus*)
Animal – Hare (*Giorria*)
Herb – Daisy (*Nóinín*)
Stone – Quartz (*Grianchloch*)

Magic and the Tree

---

1 As used by Robert Graves in *The White Goddess*, by Nigel Pennick in *The Celtic Oracle* and by Edred Thorsson – AKA Stephen Flowers.

Broom is useful for making magical tools. It actually does make a nice 'broom' to sweep an area clean in protection spells and for general use when an area needs to be cleaned before a working. It has long been used for healing, and so can be used in healing spells. The yellow blossoms are very good in this respect.

Third Aicme – Fourth Few

 The standard name for this symbol is *Straif*, pronounced 'strahf'. It is also written as *Straiph*[1]. In English, it represents the letters ST, STR or Z. The tree associated with this symbol is the Blackthorn, also known as Sloe, *Prunus spinosa*. This is one of the Shrub trees.

Kennings:

Morann Mac Main – "strongest of red, for in the sloe red for dying the things is stronger, for it is it that makes the pale silver become azure, making it genuine (?) silver. It is it, which is boiled through the urine into the white gold so as to make it red."
Mac ind Óic – "increasing of secrets."
Fenius Farsaidh – "the hedge of a stream."
Cúchulainn – "seeking of clouds."
Mad Sweeney – "o little blackthorn, little thorny one; o little black sloetree."
Ellison – trouble and negativity.

Notes on the name

Both Meroney and McManus agree that this letter-name means "sulphur." Meroney feels that the first kenning has to do with the alchemical nature of sulphur. McManus feels that the only reason this letter-name is connected to Blackthorn is the third kenning, coupled with the fact that Blackthorn is commonly used as a hedge.

Associated with: English (*Irish*)

Bird – Thrush (*Stinólach*)
River Pool – (*Sruthair*)
Fortress – (*Streulae*)
Color – Bright (*Sorcha*)
Agriculture – Flail (*Sust*)
Art – Deer-stalking (*Streghuindeacht*)
Saint – Strannan
Animal – Stallion (*Stail*)
Herb – Strawberry (*Sú talún*)
Stone – Tin (*Stan*)

---

1 As used by Edred Thorsson – AKA Stephen Flowers.

Magic and the Tree

This tree has always had the reputation for problems and trouble. There is an Old English verse that goes, "Green grows the leaves on the Blackthorn tree, we jangle and we wrangle and we never can agree."

The Romans made a tea with the leaves as a charm against witches and put the leaves in cradles to protect newborns. It has also been used on ships as protection from storms and lightning. This is another seasonal tree. It was said that if it was brought into the house when it was flowering in April and May, bad luck would follow it. This tree was often used to make staves, shillelaghs, but could only be cut for the purpose after Samhain, November 1; otherwise, the spirits of the tree would be angry.

We can use it in our magic for protection, repelling and dissolution spells. For protection, it can be added to incense or put into a protection bag placed near a bed or in your room. For repelling, it can be used as the wood a talisman is drawn on or by tying three of the sticks together while reciting the spell. For a dissolution spell, the thorn can be used either in a candle spell or in a sachet.

Third Aicme – Fifth Few

 The standard name for this symbol is *Ruis*, pronounced 'rhos'. In English, it represents the letter R. The tree associated with this symbol is the Elderberry, also known as Elder, *Sambucus nigra*. This is one of the Shrub trees. This tree should not be confused with Box Elder, often simply referred to as Elder, *Acer negundo*.

Kennings:

Morann Mac Main – "intensest of blushes, from the reddening or shame according to fact, for by 'R' it is written, and it is a reddening that grows in a man's face through the juice of the herb being rubbed under it. An ingot of a blush, again from shame or from reddening."
Mac ind Óic – "redness of faces, to wit, sap of the rose, which causes the redness of faces, so that blushing, is in them. From the blush or from the reddening."
Fenius Farsaidh – "the redness of shame"
Cúchulainn – "glow of anger."
Mad Sweeney – Not talked about.
Ellison – entrance to the Otherworld and dealings with the Fair Folk.

Notes on the name

Both Meroney and McManus agree that this letter-name means "red" or "redness." The connection to the tree comes from its property as a red dye, from the berries.

Associated with: English (*Irish*)

Bird – Small Rook (*Rócnat*)
River Pool – (*Rye*)
Fortress – (*Roigne*)
Color – Red (*Ruadh*)
Agriculture – Basket (*Rusc*)
Art – Dispensing (*Ronnaireacht*)
Saint – Ruadhan
Animal – Seal (*Rón*)
Herb - Eyebright (*Roisnin*)
Stone – Ruby (*Rúibín*)

Magic and the Tree

Along with its many medicinal uses, Elderberry was also used in spells dealing with the spirit world. In England, it was believed that if leafy branches were brought into a house, ghosts would surely follow. In Scotland, Elderberry branches were kept over the outside of the door to keep evil spirits from entering the house and a branch was placed into a coffin to keep witches from taking the body.[1] Flowers and leaves from the Elder were considered an essential part of house blessing charms.

It is thought that tree spirits inhabit all of the trees and that before taking the wood for any purpose, you should ask the permission of the spirit and explain how the wood is going to be used.

In Wales, this plant is called *"Llysan gwaed gwyn,"* (pronounced KLUH-san GOO-ide GOO-in) the "plant of the blood of man," and is considered a faerie tree. It is said that stunted trees only grow on places were human blood has been spilt. Other names for it include 'Wise Old Woman of the Hedgerow," *"Owd Gal,"* and "Elder Flower Mother.

We can use elderberry in our magic in general protection spells, spells to work with the Faerie realm and in spells dealing with psychic attacks.

---

[1] Vitale, Alice Thomas. *Leaves In Myth, Magic and Medicine.* Stewart, Tabori & Chang, NY. 1997. ISBN – 1-55670-554-9. Page 124.

Fourth Aicme

Fourth Aicme – First Few

The standard name for this symbol is *Ailm*, pronounced 'ahlm'. It is also written as *Ailim*[1]. In English, it represents the letter A. The tree associated with this symbol is the Silver Fir, *Abies alba*. This is one of the Chieftain trees. The 4th aicme are sometimes shown as dots on the line as well as the full line across, especially when written on stone.

Kennings:

Morann Mac Main – "loudest of groanings, that is wondering with him; for it is ailm or 'A' a man says while groaning in disease, or wondering, that is, marveling at whatever circumstance."
Mac ind Óic – "beginning of an answer, for the first expression of every human being after his birth is 'A'."
Fenius Farsaidh – "a fir tree, to wit, a pine tree."
Cúchulainn – "beginning of calling."
Mad Sweeney – not talked about.
Ellison – far seeing and knowing the future.

Notes on the name

This is another letter-name whose origins are troublesome. The kennings all point to the sound the letter makes, not the actual meaning of the word. As McManus says,

> "The meaning and origin of ailm remains a mystery; the glossators' 'pine- (or fir-) tree' and the derivation from palma are about as trustworthy as the rest of the arboreal fictions..."[2]

Associated with: English (*Irish*)

Bird – Lapwing (*Aidhircleóg*)
River Pool – (*Aru*)
Fortress – (Æ (*Cualand*))
Color – Piebald (*Alad*)
Agriculture – Plough (*Arathar*)

---

1 As used by Nigel Pennick in *The Celtic Oracle*.
2 McManus, Damien. *Irish Letter Names and Their Kennings*. Ériu, XXXIX (1988). Page 161.

Art – Sovereignty (*Airigeacht*)
Saint – Aed
Animal – Donkey (*Asal*)
Herb – Aconite (*Acaint*)
Stone – Amethyst (*Aimitis*)

Magic and the Tree

Being a tall tree that grows on hilltops, the fir attracts storms and lightning. It has often been used in spells to bring the rain. In Russia, three men would climb a large fir tree, one with a kettle, to imitate thunder, one with two burning sticks, to imitate lightning and one to sprinkle water to imitate rain.

In many areas, the fir tree is one of the oldest in the forest and so they are considered the grandfather and grandmother trees. The cones have long been associated with fertility spells.

We can use the fir in our magic in spells dealing with the weather or fertility and in rituals for the ancestors.

Fourth Aicme – Second Few

The standard name for this symbol is *Onn*, pronounced 'uhn'. In English, it represents the letter O. The tree associated with this symbol is the Gorse, also known as Furze, *Ulex europaeus*. This is one of the Herb trees.

Kennings:

Morann Mac Main – "helper of horses, to wit, the onnaid of the chariot, i.e. the wheels, to wit, that is onn, furze, with him, for it is by onn, 'O', that the wheels of the chariot are written. Aliter, comguinidech, equally wounding."
Mac ind Óic – "smoothest of work."
Fenius Farsaidh – "*onn*, that is furze."
Cúchulainn – "sustaining (equipment) of hunting/warrior bands."
Mad Sweeney – not talked about.
Ellison – collecting things to you.

Notes on the name

This is another of the letter-names where Meroney and McManus disagree. Meroney feels that the original meaning is wheel, while McManus feels that it is the ash tree, based in part by the description of the ash in Mad Sweeney.

Associated with: English (*Irish*)

Bird – Scrat (?) (*Odoroscrach*)
River Pool – (*Eobul*)
Fortress – (*Odba*)
Color – Dun (*Odhar*)
Agricultural – Hammer (*Ord*)
Art – Harvesting (*Ogmoracht*)
Saint – Oena
Animal – Sheep (*Óisc*)
Herb – Onion (*Oinniún*)
Stone – Gold (*Or*)

Magic and the Tree

Gorse is a favorite import to both coasts of the US, because of its property of holding sand together and drawing things to it with its roots. In English folk lore, the gorse was one of the seasonal plants that reminded people when things could be done. The rhyme for it is:

"When Gorse is out of bloom, kissing is out of season."[1]

In our magic, we can use gorse in seasonal love spells and in spells that draw things together.

---

1 Friend, Hilderic. *Flower Lore*. Para research, Inc. Rockport, MA. 1981. ISBN 0-914918-32-X. Page 216.

Fourth Aicme – Third Few

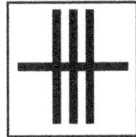
The standard name for this symbol is *Úr*, pronounced 'oor'. It is also written as *Ura*[1] and *Ur*[2]. In English, it represents the letter U. The tree associated with this symbol is the Heather, *Calluna vulgaris*. This is one of the Herb trees.

Kennings:

Morann Mac Main – "in cold dwellings, that is *ur*, fresh, with him, for from *uir*, the mould of the earth is the name derived."
Mac ind Óic – "growing of plants, that is *ur*, heath, 'U' with him, for it is *uir*, the soil of the earth, that causes the growing of the plants that are put into it."
Fenius Farsaidh – "*Ur*, that is, heath."
Cúchulainn – "shroud of a lifeless one."
Mad Sweeney – not talked about.
Ellison – healing and homelands.

Notes on the name

Both Meroney and McManus agree that the original meaning of this letter-name is earth, soil, or humus.

Associated with: English (*Irish*)

Bird – Lark (*Uiseóg*)
River Pool – (*Uissen*)
Fortress – (*Usney*)
Color – Resinous (*Usgdha*)
Agricultural – Heather- brush (*Usca*)
Art – Brass work (*Umaideacht*)
Saint – Ultan
Animal – Lamb (*Uan*)
Herb – Byrony (*Unach*)
Stone – Copper (*Umha*)

Magic and the Tree

We use this useful plant in magical spells in three ways. First, in the form of the ale made from it; second, for its connections with the faeries; and last

---
1 As used by Robert Graves in *The White Goddess*.
2 As used by Nigel Pennick in *The Celtic Oracle* and by Edred Thorsson – AKA Stephen Flowers.

in constructing magical tools. A small broom made from heather can be used to sweep an area where magic is to be preformed. The ale can be used in spells dealing with friendship or ancestral homelands. In addition, the plant itself, especially the sweet smelling blooms, can in used in incense or spells involving the Fair Folk.

Fourth Aicme – Fourth Few

 The standard name for this symbol is *Eadhadh*, pronounced 'edath'. It is also written as *Eadha*[1] and *Edad*[2] . In English, it represents the letter E. The tree associated with this symbol is the Aspen, *Populus tremula*. This is one of the Peasant trees.

Kennings:

Morann Mac Main – "distinguished wood for the trembling tree."
Mac ind Óic – "synonym for a friend."
Fenius Farsaidh – "horrible grief."
Cúchulainn – "brother of birch(?)"
Mad Sweeney – "the aspen a-trembling; by turns I hear its leaves a-racing—meseems 'tis the foray!"
Ellison – communication.

Notes on the name

This letter-name is another where both Meroney and McManus are unsure of the original meanings.

Associated with: English (*Irish*)

Bird – Swan (*Ela*)
River Pool – (*Erbus*)
Fortress – (*Naven*)
Color – Red (*Erc*)
Agriculture – Billhook (*Epit*)
Art – Fowling (*Enaireacht*)
Saint – Ernen
Animal – Eel (*Eascann*)
Herb – Hellebore (*Eileabar*)
Stone – Granite (*Eibhear*)

Magic and the Tree

The Aspen, long used in magical spells for healing, is especially favored for healing palsy. An early English spell is to pin a lock of a palsy victim's hair to an aspen tree while saying:

---

1 As used by Robert Graves in *The White Goddess* and by Nigel Pennick in *The Celtic Oracle*.
2 As used by Edred Thorsson – AKA Stephen Flowers.

> "Aspen tree, aspen tree, I prithe shiver and shake instead of me."[3]

The person would then walk away in silence or the spell would be broken. This tree is also associated with old age, due to the shivering, gossiping, and other forms of communication. Leaves carried on your person are said to facilitate your use of language.

Aspen can be used in our magic for healing and communication spells.

---

3 Vitale, Alice Thomas. *Leaves In Myth, Magic and Medicine*. Stewart, Tabori & Chang, NY. 1997. ISBN – 1-55670-554-9. Page 40.

Chapter 2 - The Tree Ogham

Fourth Aicme – Fifth Few

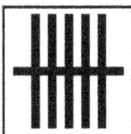

The standard name for this symbol is *Iodhadh*, pronounced 'etho'. It is also written as *Idho*[1], *Iodho*[2] and *Idad*[3]. In English, it represents the letter I. The tree associated with this symbol is the Yew, *Taxus baccata*. This is one of the Chieftain trees.

Kennings:

Morann Mac Main – "oldest of woods."
Mac ind Óic – "most withered of wood, or sword."
Fenius Farsaidh – "*ido*, that is, yew."
Cúchulainn – "energy of an infirm person (?)"
Mad Sweeney – Sweeney appears to spend more time in yew trees than he does in any other. Of it he says, "o yew-tree, little yew-tree, in churchyards thou art conspicuous."
Ellison – death and rebirth.

Notes on the name

Like the last, this is another troublesome letter-name. Whereas Meroney really is not sure what it means, McManus can see how it could be the yew tree.

Associated with: English (*Irish*)

Bird – Eaglet (?) (*Illait*)
River Pool – (*Indiurnn*)
Fortress – (*Islay*)
Color – Very White (*Irfind*)
Agriculture – Anvil (*Indeoin*)
Art – Fishing (*Iascaireach*)
Saint – Ita
Animal – Salmon (*Iach*)
Herb – Hyssop (*Iosóip*)
Stone – Iron (*Iarann*)

Magic and the Tree

This tree, known as an ancestor tree, will in many parts of Europe, be found

---
1 As used by Robert Graves in *The White Goddess*.
2 As used by Nigel Pennick in *The Celtic Oracle*.
3 As used by Edred Thorsson – AKA Stephen Flowers, and by Michael Everson.

Ogham: The Secret Language of the Druids

growing in graveyards. The trees there will usually be very old. It is the favorite wood to be used in English longbows and as such has many martial associations.

In our magic, we can use the yew is spells dealing with divination, the ancestors, re-birth, death, and for its power to cast an arrow a great distance, with strength.

Fifth Aicme

The 5th aicme, also known as the diphthongs or *Forfeda* (additional letters), is not used in some divination systems because they were not part of the original Oghams. They were added later to fit the new sounds that were coming into the Irish language. Most systems do not associate trees with them, but in my system I have, based on the Primer.

Fifth Aicme – First Few

 The standard name for this symbol is *Éabhadh*, pronounced 'eb-ath'. It is also written as *Ebad*[1] and *Ébad*[2]. In English, it represents the letters EA, CH, E or K. The tree associated with this symbol is the White Poplar, *Populus alba*. This is one of the Shrub trees.

Kennings:

Morann Mac Main –

> "most buoyant of wood, to wit, that is *ebad*, aspen, with him, for fair swimming is wood: to wit, that is a name for the great raven. Hence it was put for the letter named the Ogham *ebad*, for 'É' is a name for salmon, and it is written by 'EA' like the alphabet of the fauna: i.e., by stag (deer), 'EO' by *eonasc* (ousel)."

Mac ind Óic – "corrective of a sick man."
Fenius Farsaidh – "*Ebhadh*, that is, aspen."
Cúchulainn – "fairest fish."
Mad Sweeney – While he does not talked about White Poplar specifically, his reference to Aspen may refer to this tree as well.
Ellison – buoyancy and fl oating above problems.

Notes on the name

Neither Meroney nor McManus are sure about what the original meaning of this letter-name was, but both feel that it likely was salmon.

Associated with: English (*Irish*)

---

1 As used by Edred Thorsson – AKA Stephen Flowers.
2 As used by Michael Everson.

The associations are not usually listed in the other Oghams for the Forfeda, so are not included here.

Magic and the Tree

In several of the European countries, people plant this tree on the birth of a daughter as a dowry, giving it a folk name as a birth tree. In one of the labors of Hercules, the killing of the oxen of Geryon, he crowned himself with a wreath made of poplar leaves. He was still wearing it when he went into the Underworld and as a result, the poplar has remained silver on the top and blackened on the bottom.

In our magic, we can use the leaves and wood of the White Poplar for birth spells and in spells to attract money. It is also used in success spells and as incense for funerals or times of passing.

Chapter 2 - The Tree Ogham

Fifth Aicme – Second Few

 The standard name for this symbol is *Ór*, pronounced 'or'. It is also written as *Oir*[1]. In English, it represents the letters OI. The tree associated with this symbol is the Spindle, *Euonymus europaeus*. This is one of the Shrub trees.

Kennings:

Morann Mac Main – "most venerable of structures according to fact."
Mac ind Óic – Not given.
Fenius Farsaidh – "*Oir*, that is, spindle-tree."
Cúchulainn – No kennings listed for the rest.
Mad Sweeney – No kennings listed for the rest.
Ellison – community and working within the home.

Notes on the name

Both Meroney and McManus feel that the original meaning of this letter-name was gold.

Magic and the Tree

The spindle is one of the utilitarian trees; we use this tree for its hardness and its ability to wear well. We can use this ability in our spells whenever a long lasting spell is needed. One good way to incorporate this is by writing the spell on a piece of spindle wood.

---

1 As used by Edred Thorsson – AKA Stephen Flowers.

Fifth Aicme – Third Few

The standard name for this symbol is *Uilleann*, pronounced 'ulanth'. It is also written as *Uileand*[1] and *Uilen*[2]. In English, it represents the letters UI. The tree associated with this symbol is the European Honeysuckle, also known as woodbine, *Lonicera xylosteum*. This tree is one of the Shrub trees.

Kennings:

Morann Mac Main – "juicy wood is woodbine, that is woodbine with him, for it is a name for honeysuckle"
Mac ind Óic – "great equal length, to wit, woodbine, i.e., honeysuckle"
Fenius Farsaidh – "*Uilleand*, that is, honeysuckle."
Ellison – drawing things together and binding

Notes on the name

Both Meroney and McManus feel that the original meaning of this letter-name was elbow.

Magic and the Tree

In Scotland, farmers would place the branches of the honeysuckle in their cowsheds at Beltaine, May 1, to keep the cows from being bewitched. Honeysuckle has the property of pulling things together and forming almost impenetrable hedgerows. This property makes it very useful in spells dealing with tying or binding things together.

In our magic, we can use honeysuckle in protection spells and in binding spells.

---

1 As used by Edred Thorsson – AKA Stephen Flowers.
2 As used by Michael Everson.

Fifth Aicme – Fourth Few

The standard name for this symbol is *Ifín*, pronounced 'ibin'. It is also written as *Iphin*[1]. In English, it represents the letters IO. The tree associated with this symbol is the Gooseberry, *Ribes grossularia*. This is one of the Herb trees. This symbol has been shown drawn facing both left and right, so either is correct, and it has been shown drawn with either 2 or 4 cross lines.

Kennings:

Morann Mac Main – "sweetest of wood"
Mac ind Óic – "most wonderful of taste"
Fenius Farsaidh – "*Iphin* (pronounced 'ibin'), that is gooseberry."
Ellison – the Kindreds, especially of Nature

Notes on the name

While both Meroney and McManus are not sure of the original meaning of this letter-name, they both feel that it could have been gooseberry.

Magic and the Tree

Gooseberry is a plant that is very much favored by the spirits of nature and the faeries. Its berry is very delicious and is used as a food source by many birds and animals. In our magic, we can use the berries in spells involving the nature spirits and the thorny stems in spells involving protection.

---

1 As used by Edred Thorsson – AKA Stephen Flowers.

Fifth Aicme – Fifth Few

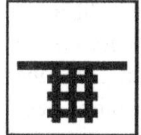

The standard name for this symbol is *Eamhancholl*, pronounced 'eman-kol'. It is also written as *Phagos*[1] and *Emancholl*[2]. In English, it represents the letters AE. The tree associated with this symbol is the Witchhazel, *Hamamelis mollis*. This tree is one of the Shrub trees. This figure has been shown drawn both above and below the line, usually above the line (not as depicted here).

Kennings:

Morann Mac Main – "expression of a weary one, i.e., ach, ah! uch, alas! That is *emancoll*, 'AE', with him, for *emancoll* is taken for ach, though it may be taken for something else"
Mac ind Óic – not given
Fenius Farsaidh – not given
Ellison – magic and hidden knowledge

Notes on the name

Both Meroney and McManus feel that the original meaning for this letter-name was "double or twinned C," based on the shape of the few.

Magic and the Tree

This tree has long been used for its binding properties, usually as an astringent to stop bleeding. In magical spells, Witchhazel can be used effectively in binding spells either as a powder or as twigs. Its property of flowering in the fall when other trees are losing their leaves can be used magically as well. In this case, it will be used when a spell is needed that is the reverse of normal use.

---

1 As used by Edred Thorsson – AKA Stephen Flowers.
2 As used by Michael Everson.

My Additions

Sixth Aicme – First Few

I've added the 6th aicme in my system as well to be used as modifiers. This is not found normally in the Ogham systems. The tree I have chosen to represent this symbol is the Norway Maple, *Acer platanoides*. In Modern Irish, this is known as *Mailp*, pronounced 'malp'. I use this Ogham in divinations as a modifier for the land. In other words, if this is drawn in a three Ogham draw, I will draw one more and know that the meanings of all the Oghams are shaded, or infl uenced by the land.

Magic and the Tree

It is thought that this tree was used by the early Celts to keep the dead from walking. In one of the Hallstead burials, the skeleton was found to be wearing shoes made of Norway maple wood. The interesting thing is that the shoes were on the wrong feet. This is usually a sign that people wanted to be sure they were not bothered by a restless spirit.

There are stores about children being passed through its branches for long life and fertility from up to almost modern times.

In our magic, we can use the maple in spells dealing with the dead, fertility and long life.

Sixth Aicme – Second Few

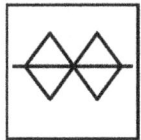

The tree I've chosen to represent this symbol is the Rush (Reed), *Phragmites australis*. In Modern Irish, this is known as *Brobh*, pronounced 'brov'. I use this Ogham in divinations as a modifier for the sea.

Magic and the Tree

The reed is useful in magic spells that deal with shape changing and with spells involving heavy trance work. Powdered and placed in incense, it is very effective in trance work.

Sixth Aicme – Third Few

The tree I've chosen to represent this symbol is the Bird Cherry, *Prunis padus*. In Modern Irish, this is known as *Craobh Fhiodhag*, pronounced 'kriv fi-dag'. I use this Ogham in divinations as a modifier for the sky.

Magic and the Tree

This tree is useful to the creatures of the fields it is found in as a source of food. We can use this in our magic when we are crafting spells that deal with the spirits of nature and especially with spells that incorporate the use of birds. The flowers of this tree, while very pretty, give off a fairly unpleasant smell. They can be used in repulsion spells or deception spells.

Other Symbols Used

Another symbol used in Ogham is the feather or arrow, which is used to show the direction to be read. The standard name for this symbol is *Eite* and it may be known as *Saighead*[1].

The last symbol used in Ogham is the space. It has been shown as both a single and a double mark. The standard name for the space is *Spás* and may be known as *Bearna*[2].

---

1 As used by Michael Everson.

3
Other Oghams from the Scholar's Primer

What follows are the oghams that most people never hear about. To me, these oghams are the heart of the "secret language" of the Druids. The tales tell us that a student in the old Druid schools would have learned all 122 ogham forms in the first year of their learning, along with 150 verse forms of poetry!

At the end of that first year, a student could expect to be asked by their teacher to compose a poem in any one of the 150 verse forms and then to write it in any one of the 122 oghams. They would then be required to compose and write it on the spot! I cannot think of anyone today who could do that.

Some of the records show that there were 150 forms of ogham that needed to be learned in the first year but I have not found the remaining 28. Therefore, the search is not over yet!

All Irish given below is in Old Irish. The translations have been taken from The Scholar's Primer, pages 289 to 313. The pictures used are from the Book of Ballymote - f.169r, 169v, 170r and 170v and are used with permission from the Royal Irish Academy. Good quality pictures of these manuscript pages can also be found at the site of "Irish Scripts On Screen," http://www.isos.dias.ie/english/index.html, under The Royal Irish Academy, MS23 P12. The numbers given refer to the order in which the oghams are found in the manuscript, excluding the first tree ogham.

There are eight types of other Oghams. Most of these fit in well with the seven uses of the ogham as discussed in Chapter 1, while two, the numbering lists, and tree ogham variations, appear to not fall into any of those main uses.

First, we have the lists of abbreviations and additional letters (Forfeda). These would fall in with the use of the oghams as a regular alphabet. Many of these have not been translated in the Primer. There are eight examples given in the lists from The Scholar's Primer. They are numbers: 50, 51, 52, 56, 104, 105, 106, 107, and 108.

Then we have the Secret Writing Oghams. In these, the oghams were formed in many different ways using different marks than the fews in the Tree

Ogham. There are 43 examples given in the lists from The Scholar's Primer. They are numbers: 30, 38, 39, 40, 44, 46, 55, 64, 67, 76, 77, 78, 79, 80, 81, 82, 83, 88, 89, 90, 91, 92, 93, 94, 95, 96, 97, 98, 99, 100, 101, 109, 110, 112, 113, 114, 115, 117, 118, 119, 120, and 121.

Then we have the Cipher Oghams. In these oghams, it is important to remember that the ciphers are based on Old Irish so they usually do not make too much sense unless you understand the Old Irish. There are 44 examples given in the lists from The Scholar's Primer. They are numbers: 15, 16, 25, 26, 27, 28, 29, 31, 32, 33, 34, 35, 36, 41, 42, 43, 45, 48, 49, 58, 59, 60, 61, 62, 63, 65, 66, 68, 69, 70, 71, 72, 73, 74, 75, 84, 85, 86, 87, 102, and 103.

Next, we have mnemonic lists, which are designed to help the students memorize important information, such as the names of kings. There are 11 examples given in the lists from The Scholar's Primer. They are numbers: 2, 3, 4, 5, 6, 9, 10, 21, 22, 23, & 24.

Then there are those oghams used as a gesture language. They are numbers: 18, 19 and 20, plus the shin ogham, which is not listed in the Primer, but is referred to by McManus.

Next, we have the ogham used for divination. There is only one example used in the list from The Scholar's Primer, the Boy Ogham, number 17. There are no oghams given in the lists in the Primer that are specifically referred to as being used for magic, but it is possible that any of the code or secret writing oghams could have been used for this purpose.

We end this list with the two types of oghams that do not seem to fall into any of the categories for the general uses of the oghams. First, there are the numbering lists, which may have been used as ciphers or as a memorization aid. There are 12 examples given in the lists from The Scholar's Primer with one, the Sow Ogham listed twice, with a slight variation. They are numbers: 1, 7, 8, 11, 12, 13, 14, 37, 47, 57, 111, and 116.

Last, we have the variations of the tree oghams. In these, alternate spellings are given for some of the trees. It is very possible that these are actually referring to different varieties of the trees. There are two examples given in the lists from The Scholar's Primer. They are numbers: 53 & 54.

Chapter 3 -Other Oghams from the Scholar's Primer

The *Forfeda* Lists

50) Abbreviations #1 Ogham – "Of extra groups and syllables of the ogham here according to the excessive powers whereby there are syllables, extra groups, and extra alphabets of them, etc."

> B - *bacht*, L - *lact*, F - *fect*, S - *sect*, N – *nect*
> H - *huath*, D - *drong*, T - *tect*, C - *caect*, Q – *quiar*
> M - *maei*, G - *gæth*, NG - *ngæl*, STR - *strmrect*, R – *rect*
> A - *ai*, O - *ong*, U - *ur*, E - *eng*, I – *ing*

51) Abbreviations #2 Ogham – Similar to Abbreviations #1 Ogham, number 50 above. The abbreviations are listed as: cai or æi, c or onn, p or iu, I ol on, no or no, ach ui oi ai au, air cair, s, bran, tri, bran, tru, cru, cru, Columcille, Ceallach, Cuilibadh. Also interesting in this ogham is the use of a complete set of different symbols for the fews.

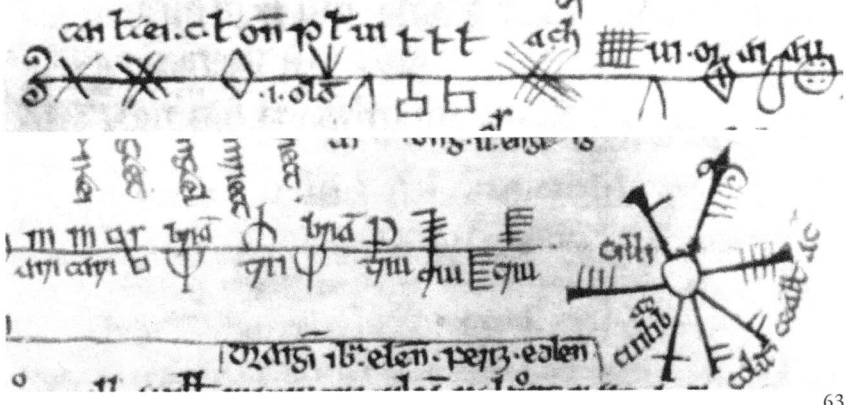

Ogham: The Secret Language of the Druids

52) Unnamed #3 Ogham – simply given as *goach, tucht, ict, miliu, eth, ean*.

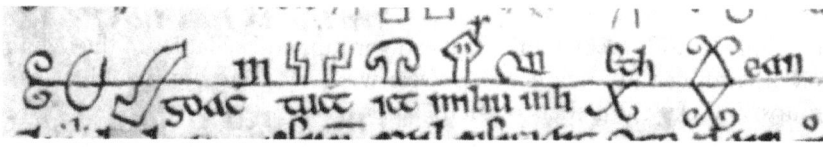

56) Not translated.

"*Saitheach fochrom, clu co mboil,
Dodaing foluaich lucht asmbit.
Brec oc forglais, derg (gl. Midoth findi 7rl.), oc find
Mælsem (gl. Ardoth findi 7rl.), fuirid (gl. Derg mæsem),
leitheal, brann (gl. Sætech).
Cruithean fororcan so sis: dodaing brec.*"

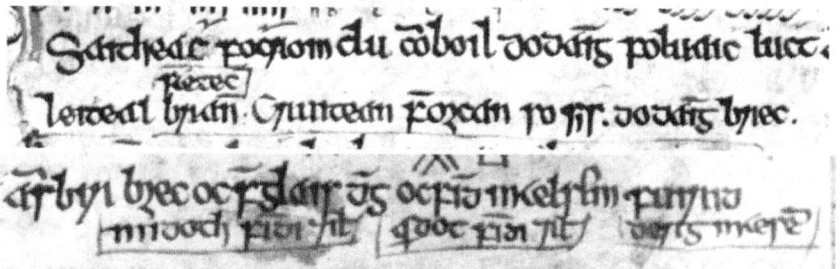

104) Abbreviations – Not translated. These abbreviations are shown as symbols drawn on the centerline.

"*iul, og, ech, ind, lii, rii, lii, ict, arb, insci, ruidriug, di alim, fict, dacht, gart.*"

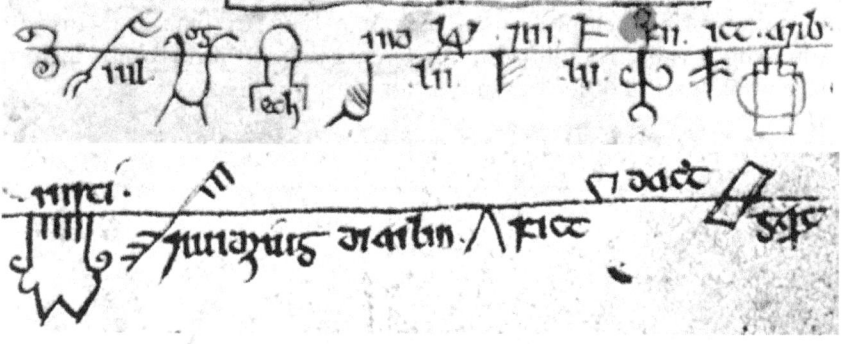

105) 10 further expressions, also drawn as symbols along the centerline.

"*tii: diailt: ban bachlach insci: maidm cridi eors: gai: eet: ara: sesd: lat: nact: dec indsci so anuas.*"

Chapter 3 - Other Oghams from the Scholar's Primer

106) *Forfeda* #1 – Additional Letters – These expressions are not translated and are shown as symbols drawn along a centerline.

> "sigan fain ailm: remar ailm: srub-aigi: troigi: trenoct: enoct: duiriu: coeliu: aupai: ui: bang: ue: gort guinche: ailm guinche."

107) *Forfeda* #2 – Additional Letters – These expressions are not translated and are shown as symbols drawn along a centerline.

> "mane: esci: goth: te: ongan: ail: dea: eth: oeth: neal: taeb: iicht: fisidect: laisairect: emridoth: maicc."

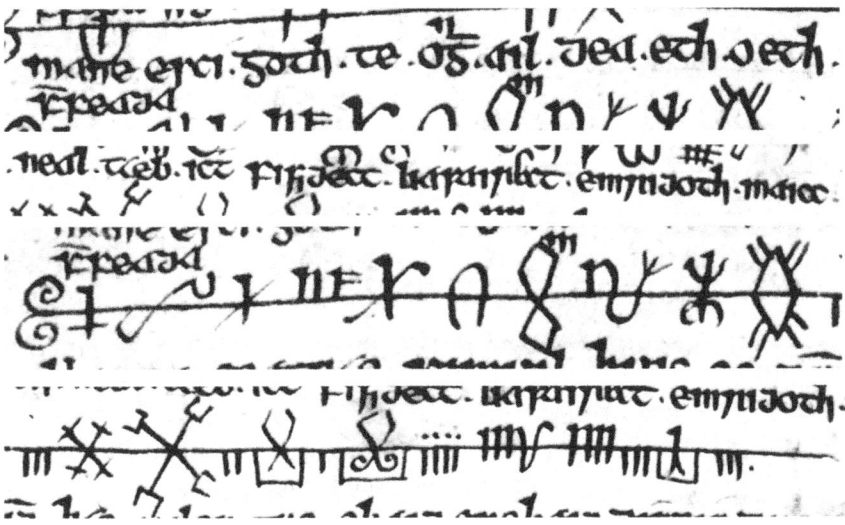

108) *Forfeda #3* – Additional Letters – These expressions are not translated and are shown as symbols drawn along a centerline.

> "uaitea: caetrae: samuil: huic: oe: dind: hæ: Uilen: tre: ebaid: enebaid: dirdin: dur: didad: fir: ailm."

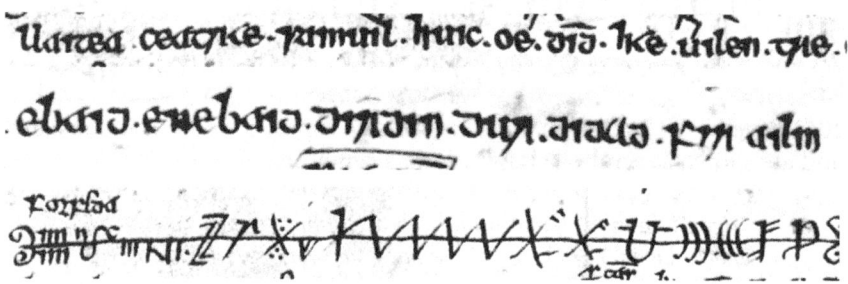

The Secret Writing Lists

30) Hinge Ogham – This ogham is different from the rest. It uses the ladder format but uses hinge shaped markings in between the parallel line with dots to the left or right of the X to indicate the few for the B and H groups. The M group is indicated by a straight-line perpendicular to the cross bar with from 1 to 5 curved lines coming up from the cross bar to meet it. The A group is small rectangles in the center of the cross bars with dots or lines to indicate which few it is. The diphthongs are written along a centerline drawn between the two parallel lines.

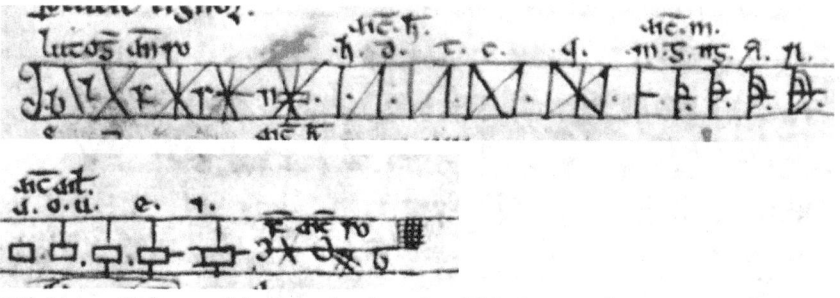

38) Secret Ogham of the Warrior-bands – This is an ogham system that uses curved lines that all flow from one to another along the stem line.

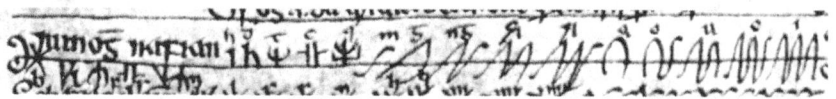

39) Unnamed of *Ilann* Ogham – This is an ogham system that is different from the rest. This is read horizontally from left to right.

Chapter 3 -Other Oghams from the Scholar's Primer

B – 1 down, L – 1 down & 1 up (up to right of down), F – 2 down & 1 up,
S – 2 down & 2 up (up to right of down), N – 3 down and 2 up
H – 1 up, D – 1 up & 1 down (up to left of down), T – 2 up & 1 down,
C – 2 up and 2 down (up to left of down), Q – 3 up & 2 down
M – 1 across, curved to right, G – 2 across, curved to right, NG – 3 across, curved to right, STR – 4 across, curved to right, R – 5 across, curved to right
A – 1 across, curved to left, O – 2 across, curved to left, U – 3 across, curved to left, E – 4 across, curved to left, I – 5 across, curved to left

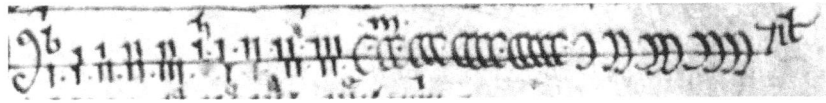

40) *Ebad*-fashioned Ogham (pronounced 'eb-ath') – This system appears to be the normal ogham with diagonal lines running from upper left to lower right crossing the fews with the fews written on them for the B and H groups. It is similar to #85 *Ebad*-fashioned Ogham

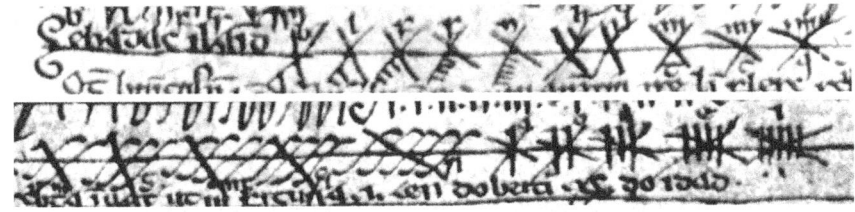

44) Letter Rack Ogham – This ogham uses vertical lines coming down or up from the centerline with cross marks on them for the symbol, i.e., B – line coming down with one cross on it, H – line going up with one cross on it, L – line coming down with two cross marks on it, etc. The M and A group are written the same way only cross the centerline.

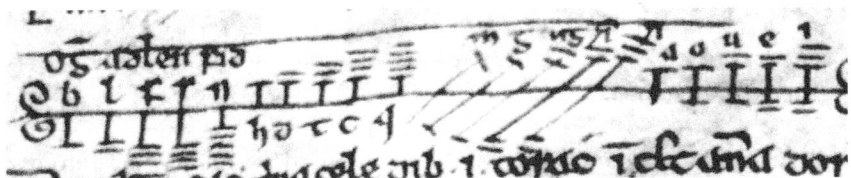

46) Anguish of a Poet's Heart Ogham – The symbols are written below or above small boxes drawn either below or above the centerline for the B and H groups. The M and A groups are mixed together.

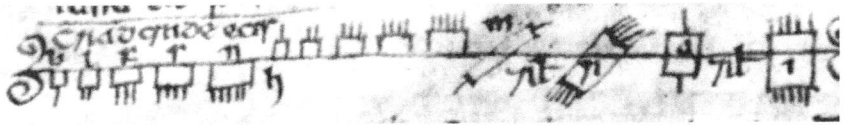

55) Unnamed #6 Ogham - This ogham uses the standard symbols with tiny flourishes to all the letters, probably another manuscript ogham.

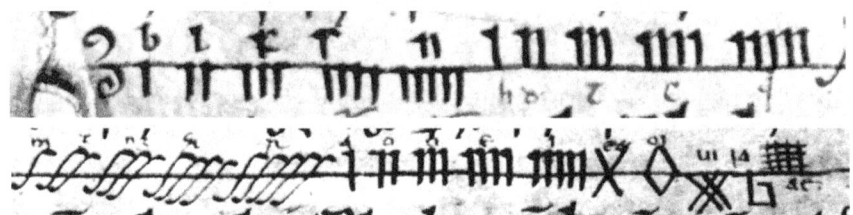

64) Enclosed Ogham – "An enclosure between every two letters, i.e., a limit only to the letter itself." The symbols are drawn with a box around the few.

67) Great Dotting Ogham – The symbols are designated by the number of dots after the letter, i.e., for the B group, B - a line to the right, followed by one dot, L – a line to the right followed by 2 dots, etc.

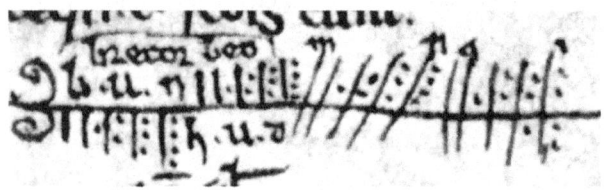

76) Lively Dotting Ogham – The symbols are written in the normal manner except that dots are placed on the few indicating the number of their position, i.e., b – 1 dot, l – 2 dots, etc. For example, for B, the few is drawn normally, then for L, the few is drawn with a line coming down with one dot on it. F is drawn with one line coming down with two dots on it, etc.

77) Strife Head Ogham – Diagonal lines are used for the B and H groups, right facing brackets are used for the M group and left facing brackets are used for the A group. The brackets cross the centerline, the diagonal lines do not.

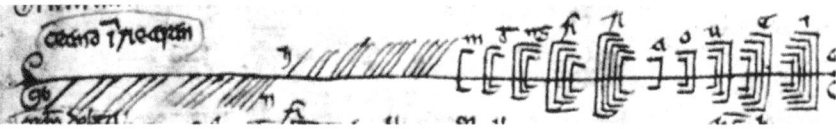

78) Ogham of Dedu – The fews have small horizontal marks on them for the position of the symbol, i.e., b – 1 mark, l – 2 marks, etc. On the M and

Chapter 3 -Other Oghams from the Scholar's Primer

A groups, the marks are divided both above and below the line, i.e., m – 1 mark above, g – 1 mark above & 1 mark below, ng – 2 marks above & 1 mark below, etc. Similar to #80 - Unnamed #8 Ogham.

79) Head of Dispute Ogham – The centerline is drawn as a line going both above and below a second centerline. The fews are placed both below, then above the second centerline.

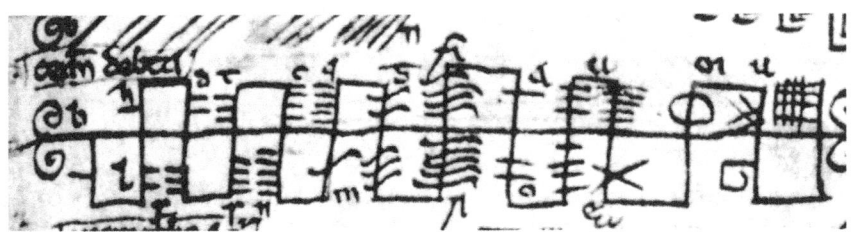

80) Unnamed #8 Ogham – Similar to the Ogham of Dedu, #78, only the marks on the fews are longer and cross the lines.

81) Infilleted Ogham – This ogham uses a completely different symbol set for the letters.

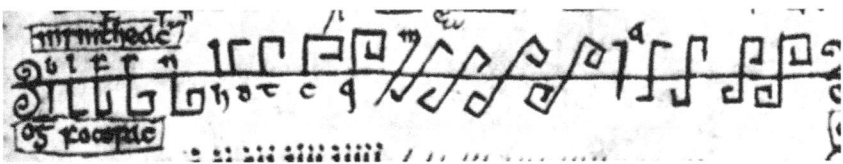

82) Ridgeless Ogham – Similar to the normal ogham but all the fews are drawn OFF the centerline. For the M and A groups, half the few is above and half below the centerline.

83) Well-footed Ogham – In this system, each of the fews have a small dot at their end, one dot for each few.

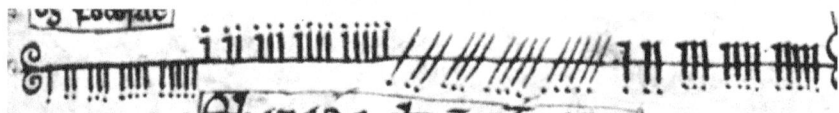

88) Side Ogham of Tlachtga – All the fews are on one side of the centerline. The B group is shown by diagonal lines starting at the centerline and going down to the left. The H group is shown by diagonal lines starting at the centerline and going down to the right. The M group is shown by diagonal lines going down and to both the right and left. And the A group is shown by straight lines going down from the centerline. There are one through five lines for all groups as usual.

89) Unnamed #9 Ogham – Here we have another ogham that uses a completely different set of markings.

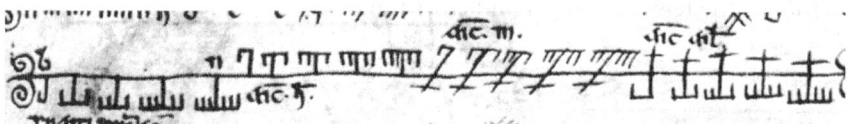

90) Ogham of Erimon – This system uses triangles drawn either above or below the centerline to represent the letters. Not all letters are represented.

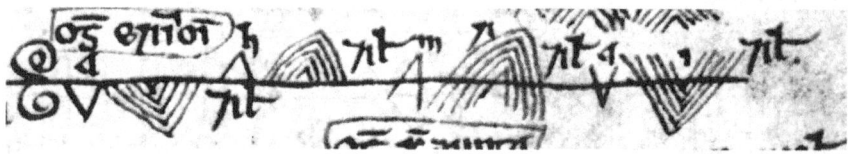

91) Interwoven Thread Ogham – All symbols are written with cross hatch lines through them, similar to UI in the diphthongs.

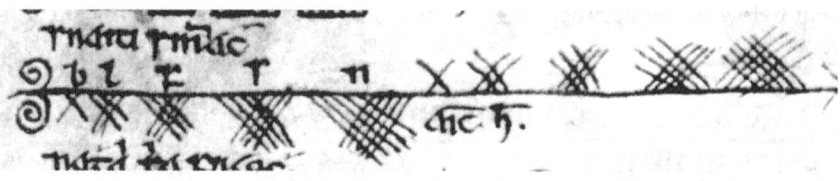

Chapter 3 -Other Oghams from the Scholar's Primer

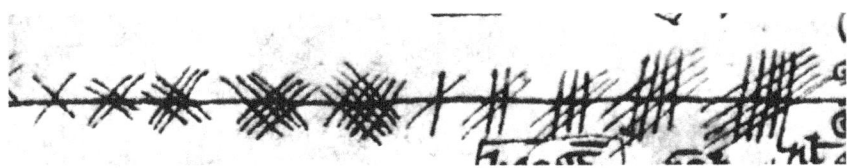

92) Fore-enclosed Ogham – With this ogham, all the symbols are written with boxes drawn around them.

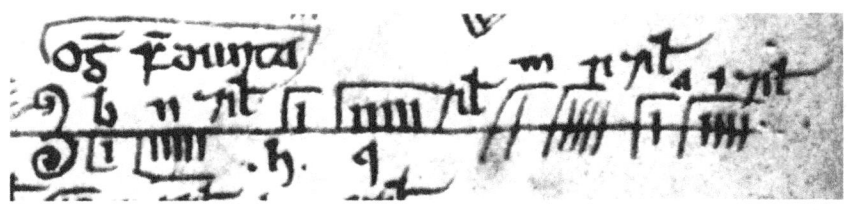

93) Snake Through Heath Ogham – This is drawn with a curving line around each of the symbols. The line is similar to humps above and below the centerline around each of the symbols. This system is similar to #110 – Rope Ogham.

94) Bend (or Angle) Ogham – The symbols for this ogham are all written with bends in the fews, i.e., B would be written with a stroke down from the centerline, a sharp bend to the left for a short distance, then a sharp bend down again.

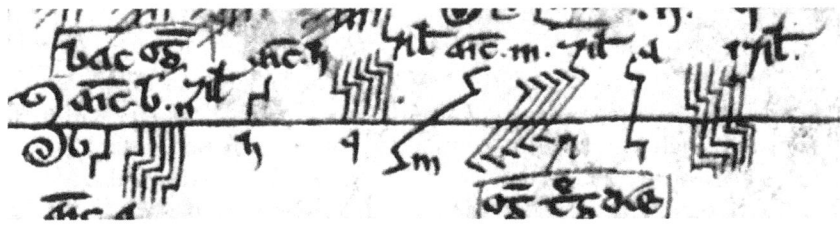

95) Unnamed #10 Ogham – In this symbol set, the B and H groups are written inside triangles, each few within its own triangle. The M and A groups are written inside boxes, each few within its own box.

96) Pierced Ogham – These symbols are drawn with a cross line, parallel to the centerline through the fews.

97) Unnamed #11 Ogham – These symbols are drawn with two lines meeting in the middle of the few, similar to a 'peace sign'.

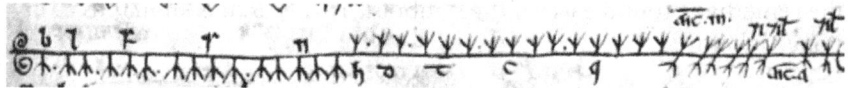

98) Place Ogham – In this set, all the fews are drawn with boxes around them.

99) Tooth-like Ogham of Fionn – "And it is for brevity that there are two letters of every group written." All groups only use symbols 1 & 5. Group B is drawn through the centerline with a box covering the bottom half of the fews, i.e., below the centerline only. Group H is drawn through the centerline as well with a box covering the upper half of the few. = Group M uses chevrons, a diagonal line above and below the centerline, facing to the right. Group A uses chevrons facing to the left.

Chapter 3 - Other Oghams from the Scholar's Primer

100) Shield Ogham – The B group is written like and upside down 'V' with its point above the centerline. There is one 'V' for B, two 'V's,' inside each other, for L, etc. Group H is written similar to the B group but with the point of the 'V' on the centerline. Group M is written using chevrons placed above the centerline facing to the right. Group A is written using chevrons above the centerline facing left.

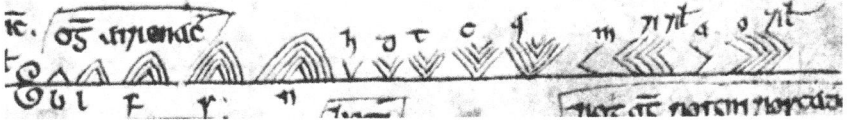

101) Wheel Ogham of Roscadach - This ogham system uses a circle divided into four quarters. Each group is written in one of the quarters as dots. One dot for B, two for L, etc. The B group starts in the upper left quadrant and the groups go clockwise from there.

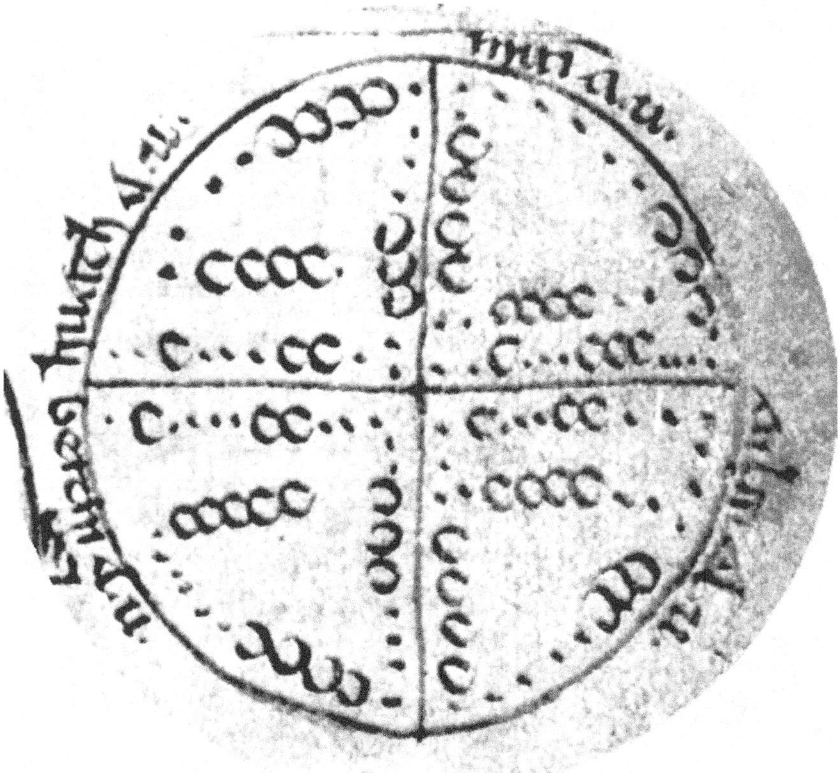

109) Oblique Ogham – In this system, the fews are written diagonally. The B group starts at the centerline and are drawn down and to the left. The H group is drawn up and to the left. The M group normally and the A group are drawn across the centerline from right above to left below.

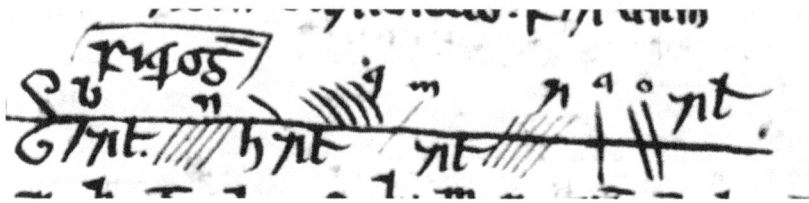

110) Strand Stream of Ferchertne Ogham – In this system, the fews are drawn between to parallel lines that form a rectangle inside another rectangle. Different symbols are used than the standard ogham. Similar to #103 – Stream strand of Ferchertne above but uses only two rectangles instead of four. This is written around Other Ogham #111.

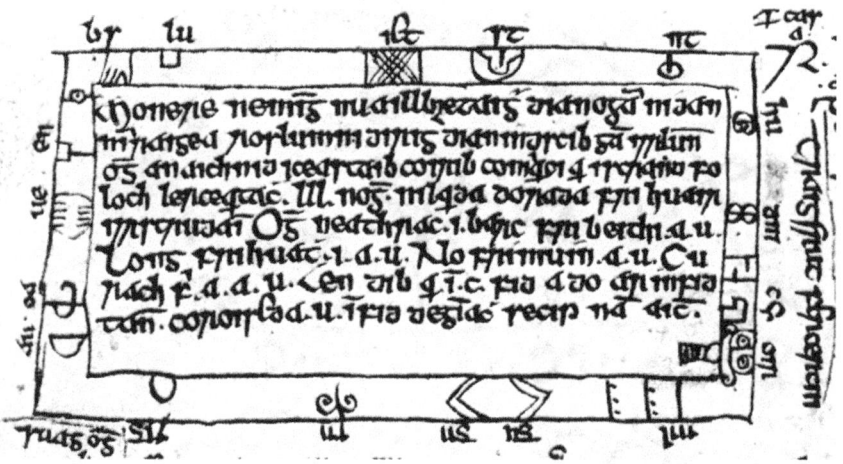

112) Egyptian (Hebrew) Ogham – This system uses Hebrew letters (?) for the symbols.

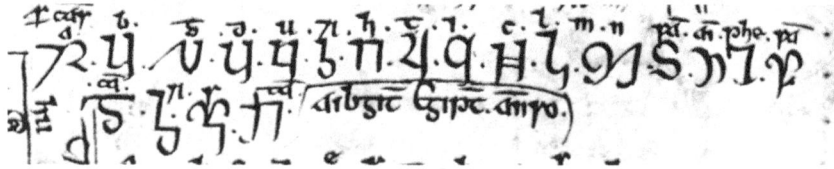

113) Unnamed #12 Ogham – This system uses another symbol set for the oghams. I am not sure which language the symbols come from.

Chapter 3 - Other Oghams from the Scholar's Primer

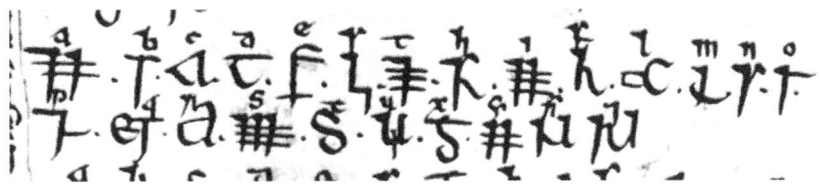

114) African Alphabet Ogham – This system uses another symbols set (African?) for the symbols.

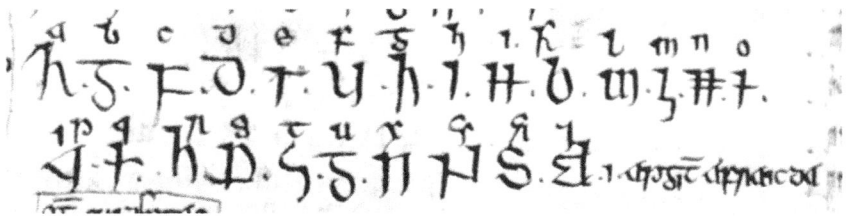

115) Rope Ogham – The centerline of this system extends above and below the centerline, enclosing each of the fews. It is similar to #93 – Snake through Heath Ogham above

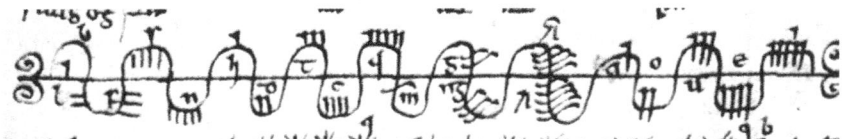

117) Unnamed #13 Ogham – This is another ogham system that uses fews with marks across them. It is similar to the Unnamed #11 Ogham, number 97 above.

118) Unnamed #14 Ogham – This system uses a caret (^) through the centerline for each few. The marks are drawn across the caret, i.e. one mark to the right from the right edge for B, one mark to the left from the left edge for H, one mark diagonally down from the right edge, toward the left, for M and one mark across the top for A.

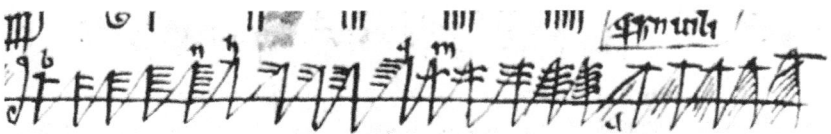

Ogham: The Secret Language of the Druids

119) Scandinavian Ogham – This system uses still a different symbols set for the fews. This is the first of the oghams with a "runic" look.

120) Viking Ogham #1 – This system uses words for the names of the letters. Only four letters from each aicme are used. The words are not translated. Symbols along the centerline are also used for this system.

    B - *fea*, L - *ar*, F - *turs*, S - *or*
    H - *raid*, D - *caun*, T - *hagal*, C - *naun*
    M - *isar*, G - *sol*, NG - *duir*, STR - *bangann*
    A - *mann*, O - *langor*, U - *eir*

121) Viking Ogham #2 – This system uses rune-like symbols written below the centerline for the symbols.

The Cipher Lists

15) Blind Man Ogham – This system uses a man's name. The name is divided to the right side for the B and M groups and to the left side for the H and A groups.

16) Lame Ogham – This system is the same as Blind Man Ogham, #15 above. It uses a person's name and divides it.

Chapter 3 - Other Oghams from the Scholar's Primer

25) Head in Bush or Persisting Ogham – This is an interesting cipher ogham. "It uses the letter at the beginning of the word, i.e. as far as the name of it (the letter) resembles the beginning of whatever word it is, to write that letter at the beginning of the name for its own name; and to write the end of the name according to the proper letters." The example given in the Scholar's Primer is for *certle* – ball of thread. This is read using the *Cert* (pronounced kwurt) spelling for the letter 'Q' in Old Irish. Therefore, it would read *(cert=q)le*.

26) Head Under Bush Ogham – This is another cipher Ogham. It is the opposite of the Head in Bush Ogham, #25 above. In this ogham, "the letter at the end of the name is used to write the beginning of it according to its proper letters. The example given in the Scholar's Primer is for *Mael R*, to wit Ruis. I am not sure how they arrive at Ruis from this.

27) Serpent About Head Ogham – For this system, the Primer gives - "to write the first letter of the name in the middle of the stem, and to write the name straight thence to the end of the stem; and to write it backwards to the beginning of the stem, so that it is the same thing that stands at the beginning and at the end of the stem, i.e. it is the end of the word which stands on each of them, indifferent to read it up or down; and it is from the middle of it that the name is read, for there stands the first letter of the name." The example given in the Primer is:

This would be read from the middle as "*CELLACH*" and it reads the same both ways – HCALLECELLACH, an early palindrome. We will see a variation of this word in ogham #51.

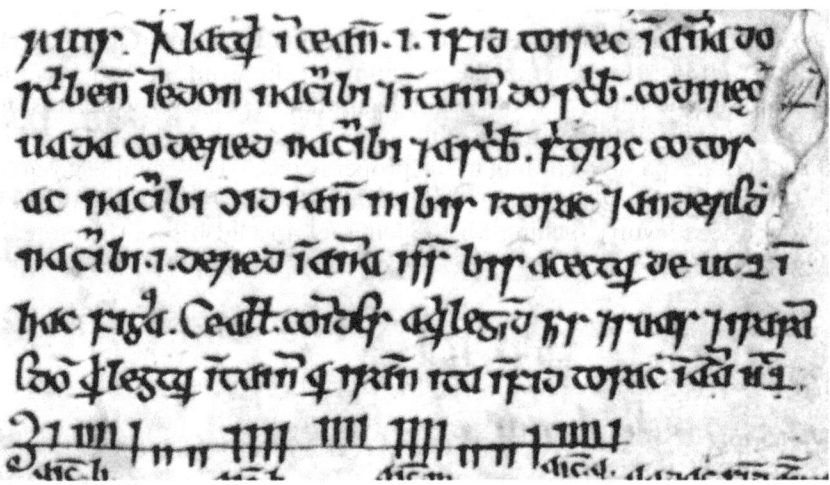

28) Ladder Ogham of Fionn – This is shown as having the form of a ladder on its side with two parallel bars with cross bars in between them. The cross bars are the few, with the markings on them, read in the usually way, B group to the right.

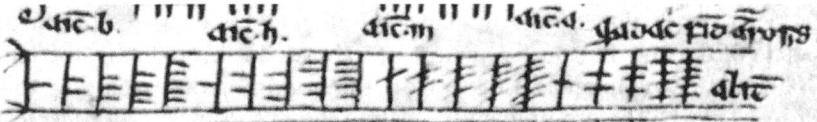

29) Diphthong Group Behind Us Ogham – This ogham is similar to the Ladder Ogham of Fionn, #28 but it has the B and H groups starting at the top and bottom, has each few enclosed and it includes the 5th aicme below the ladder as a separate but connected ladder.

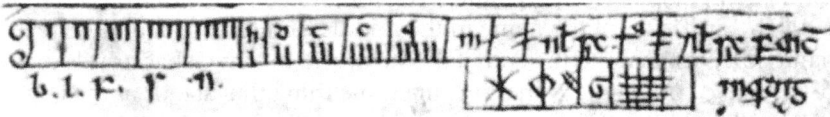

31) Three Ridged Ogham – This ogham is written along three parallel lines with the groups on all three but in different sections of the lines. The lines are drawn through the line they are on, i.e. the left side of the bottom line for the B group, the right side of the middle line for the M group, and then the A group and left side of the top line for the diphthongs, then the H group.

Chapter 3 -Other Oghams from the Scholar's Primer

32) Three-stemmed Ogham of Fionn – This is another ogham written with three parallel lines. The symbols are placed in groups of two along the line.
Top line - 2 from the B group (1 & 4), then 2 from the H group (2 & 5), then 1 from the M group (2), then 2 from the A group (1 & 4) and then 1 from the diphthongs (3).
Middle line - 2 from the B group (2 & 5), then 1 from the H group (3), then 2 from the M group (2 & 5), then 2 from the A group (2 & 5) and then 2 from the diphthongs (2 & 4).
Bottom line - 1 from the B group (3), then 2 from the H group (1 & 4), then 2 from the M group (1 & 4), then 1 from the A group (3) and then 2 from the diphthongs (1 & 5).

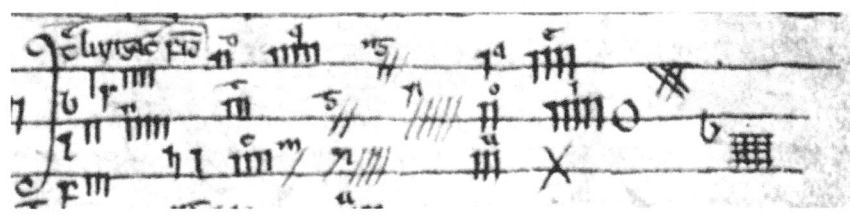

33) Canal Ogham – This is another three-ridged ogham, with the H group on the top line to the left and the rest of the groups on the centerline, B then M then A. On the bottom line are the diphthongs.

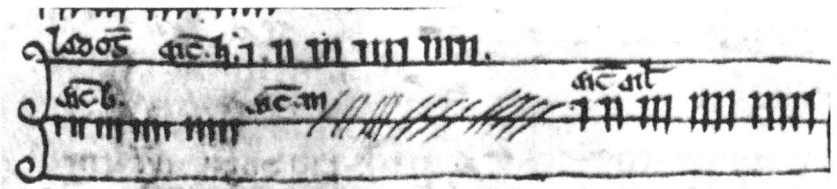

34) Unnamed #1 Ogham – Similar to the Three-stemmed Ogham of Fionn, #32 above, but the markings are in different places.
Top line - 2 from the B group (1 & 4), then 1 from the H group (3), then one from the M group (3), then 1 from the A group (3) and then 1 from the diphthongs (3).
Middle line - 2 from the B group (2 & 5), then 2 from the H group (2 & 4), then 2 from the M group (2 & 5), then 2 from the A group (2 & 4) and then 2 from the diphthongs (2 & 4).

Bottom line - 1 from the B group (3), then 2 from the H group (1 & 5), then two from the M group (1 & 4), then 2 from the A group (1 & 5) and then 2 from the diphthongs (1 & 5).

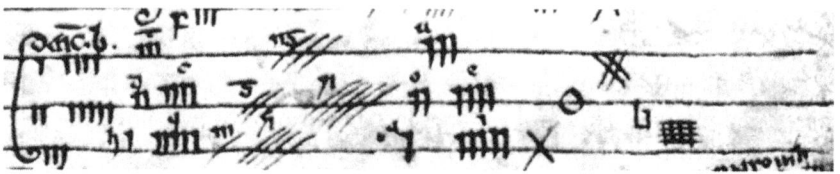

35) Four-ridged Ogham of Crutine – This is a system with four parallel lines with group B on the bottom line, group H on the top line and groups M and A going through all four of the lines.

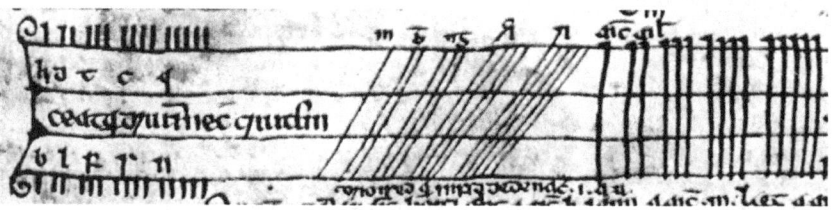

36) Aliter Ogham – Another four-ridged ogham. The B group goes through the bottom line, the H group goes through the bottom two lines, the M group goes through the bottom three lines and the A group goes through all four lines.

41) Ogham of Bricriu – "The depth in which the letters stand in the alphabet is the number of strokes that are written in its formation, i.e. one mark for b (1st aicme, 1st few) and 20 marks for i (4th aicme, 5th few)."

(See illustrations on following page)

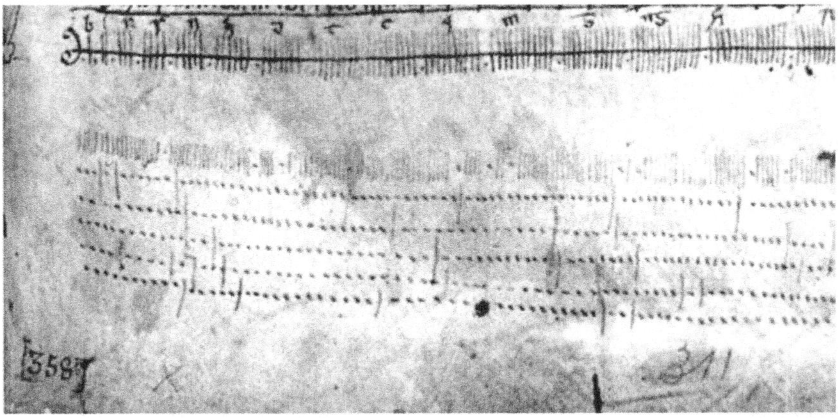

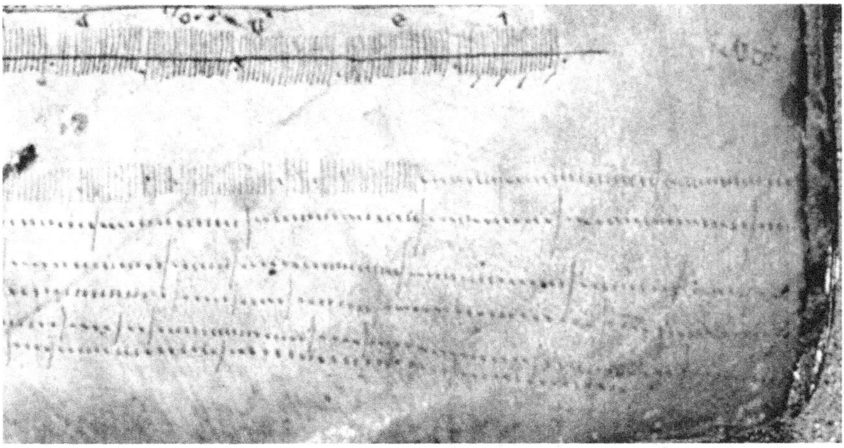

Chapter 3 -Other Oghams from the Scholar's Primer

42) Order Ogham – "The order, which the letters have in the alphabet, i.e., the letter which is earlier than another in an alphabet, is written earlier in forming the name, and the last, last in forming the name." The examples given in the Primer are Bran, written as **b** (1st) **n** (5th) **r** (15th) **a** (16th) and Labraid, written as **b** (1st) **l** (2nd) **d** (7th) **r** (15th) **a** (16th) **a** (16th) **i** (20th).

43) Unnamed #2 Ogham – "Ogham on which is one, i.e., one stroke too many to be written with each letter, etc., up to five of each."

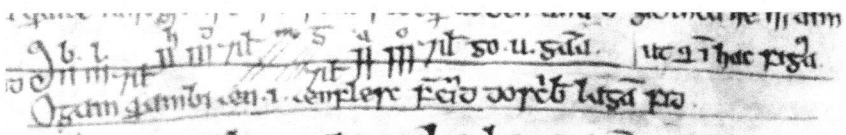

Ogham: The Secret Language of the Druids

45) Hunt-track Ogham – "i.e., two names to be written, i.e., each of them through the other, i.e., the beginning of the first name to be written up to the half of it, and the beginning of the other name after it, and the end of the first name after it, and the end of the other name after it; and wherein are names which are formed identically, those of a first name and those of a last, as they stand in the two stems there." The examples given in the Primer are bec-an, ler-an – A little, a small sea and feth-nat, seg-nat – A little calm, a small deer.

48) Conjunct Ogham – This is given in the Primer as the following with no further interpretation, "The letter that is next to the letter to be written along with it without interruption."

49) Twin Ogham – "Two identical letters are written for the letter, i.e., bb for b, hh for h, etc."

58) "The Ogham that Confused Breas, Son of Elatha." Breas was under a prohibition not to pass on without reading this ogham. This ogham was afterwards thrown into his bosom as he went to the Battle of Moytura. Afterwards he lost the battle while he was reading the ogham. This is the alphabet of this ogham, to wit, the letter is written with all the letters that stand in the person's name. Each letter, besides being written, is spelt."

Chapter 3 -Other Oghams from the Scholar's Primer

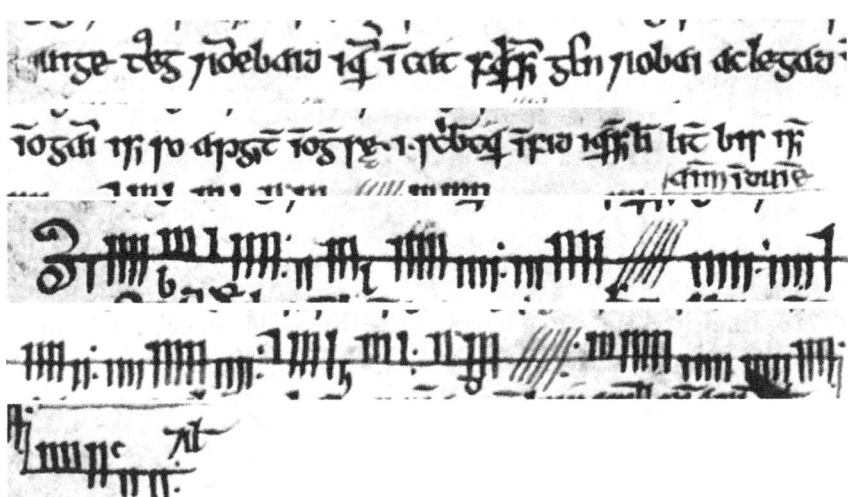

59) Final Ogham – "The last letter of the name (of the letter) is written for the letter, i.e., **e** for **b** (*beithe*), **s** for **l** (*luis*), **n** for **f** (*fern*), **l** for **s** (*sail*), **n** for **n** (*nin*), 7rl.: æ, or **cc**, or **ch**."

60) Head on Proscription Ogham – "The last letter of every group is written for the first letter, and the first letter of every group for the last letter, i.e., **n** for **b** and **b** for **n**, and every letter for its fellow in the whole group and everything to be turned all backwards into itself, **ia** or **p**: æ or **cc** or **ch**."

Ogham: The Secret Language of the Druids

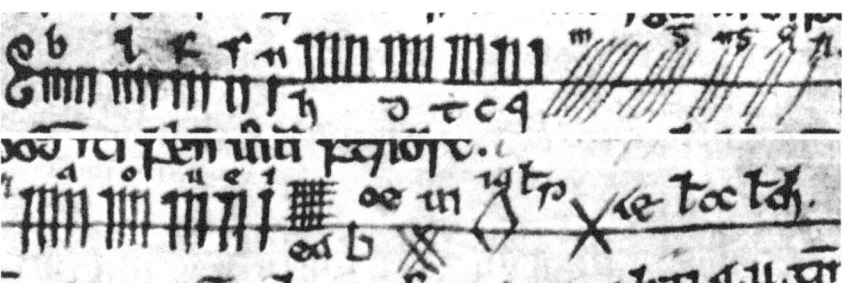

61) Foursome Ogham – Four letters only are spoken in it, i.e., d, t, l and f.
   B - d, L - dd, F - ddd, S - dddd, N – ddddd
   H - t, D - tt, T - ttt, C - tttt, Q - ttttt
   M - l, G - ll, NG - lll, STR - llll, R – lllll
   A - f, O - ff, U - fff, E - ffff, I – fffff

62) Uproar of Anger Ogham – "The first letter of every group for B, five; the second letter of every group for H, five; the third letter of every group for M, five, etc." The diphthongs are mixed in.
   B – B, L – H, F – M, S – A, N – EA
   H – L, D – D, T – G, C – O, Q – OI
   M – F, G – T, NG – NG, STR – U, R – UI
   A – S, O – C, U – STR, E – E, I – IO
   EA – N, OI – Q, UI – R, IO – I, AE – AE

Chapter 3 -Other Oghams from the Scholar's Primer

63) Point-to-eye Ogham – Similar to Mane (?) backwards, #65 below. In this ogham we find group A forwards for group B, i.e., a for b and i for n; group M backwards for group H, i.e., r for h and m for q; group B backwards for group A, i.e., b for i and n for a, and group H for group M backwards, i.e., q for m and h for r.

Calder's description of this on page 306 in the Scholar's primer really does not match the picture that describes this ogham. His description reads: "Mane (?) backwards, i.e., group A. backwards for group B. i.e., i for b and b for i; group M. for group H., i.e., r for h and h for r, etc. Group B. for group A. backwards and group H. for group M. backwards."

  B - A, L - O, F - U, S - E, N – I
  H - R, D - STR, T - NG, C - G, Q – M
  M - Q, G - C, NG - T, STR - D, R – H
  A - N, O - S, U - F, E - L, I – B

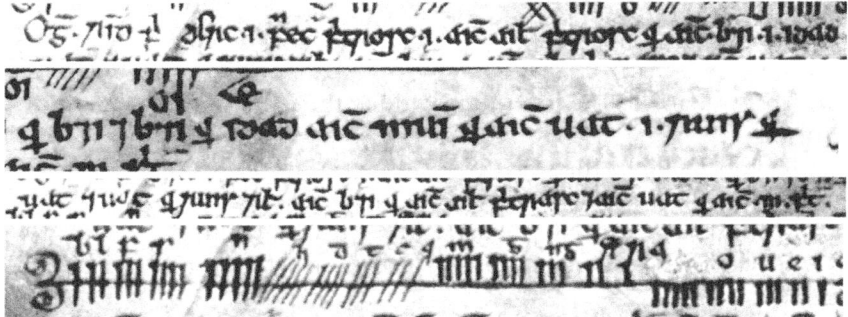

65) Mane (?) Backwards Ogham – The symbols are drawn in reverse order, including the diphthongs, i.e., 5th aicme, group A, group M, group H then group B. The number of marks are reversed as well, i.e., 5, 4, 3, 2, 1. See also #63 above.

66) Unnamed #7 Ogham – Each of the symbols except the last are drawn with the first letter of the group after them, i.e. B, B, then L, B, then F, B, etc for all the symbols but the fifth in each group.

Ogham: The Secret Language of the Druids

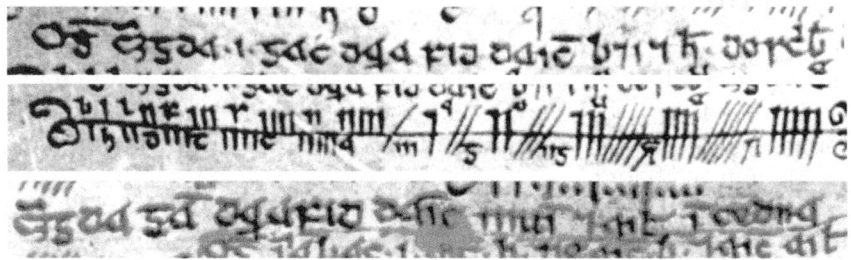

68) Mixed Ogham – Every second letter of groups B and H to be written mixed; then every second letter of groups M and A. For example, B, H, L, D, F, T, S, C, N, Q.

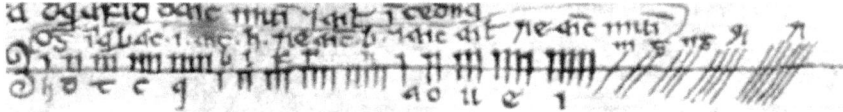

69) Combative Ogham – "Group H before group B and group A before group M."

H - H, D - D, T - T, C - C, Q – Q
B - B, L - L, F - F, S - S, N – N
A - A, O - O, U - U, E - E, I - I
M - M, G - G, NG - NG, STR - STR, R - R

70) Host Ogham – "The letter to be written thrice for itself, i.e., b thrice, l thrice, etc."

B - bbb, L - lll, F - fff, S - sss, N – nnn
H - hhh, D - ddd, T - ttt, C - ccc, Q – qqq
M - mmm, G - ggg, NG - ngngng, STR - strstrstr, R – rrr
A - aaa, O - ooo, U - uuu, E - eee, I – iii

71) End to End Ogham – "The two ends of the stem to be joined, i.e., group A to be mixed backwards with group B, i.e., i between b and l, etc.; group M to be mixed with group H. The extra groups similarly."

Chapter 3 -Other Oghams from the Scholar's Primer

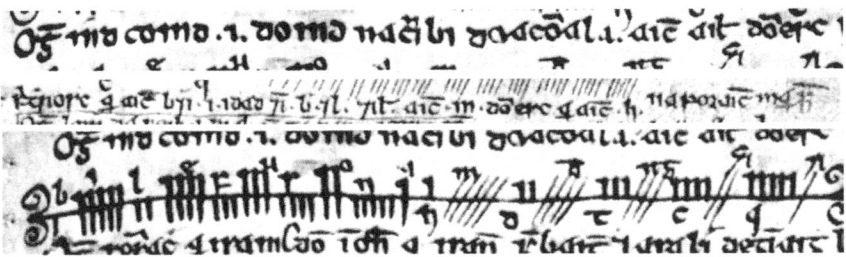

72) Two Stoke Ogham – A stroke is written between each letter.

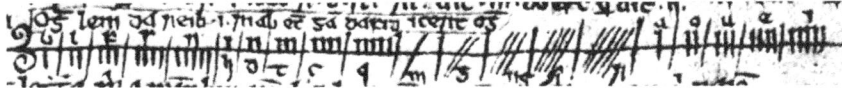

73) Steadfast Ogham – "For its middle is the same, for there it is completed, and from its latter half it is read *prius* (first), for there are the B and H groups, for in its middle is the completion of the four groups."
M, G, NG, STR, R
A, O, U, E, I
Q, C, T, D, H
N, S, F, L, B

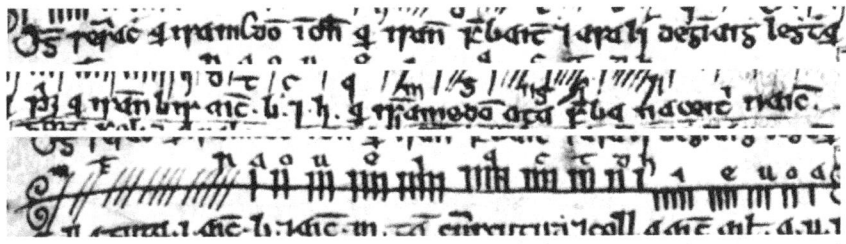

74) Corn-field Ogham – "Corn-field under color, that there might not be two ogham letters for one letter, i.e., three letters between every two letters of group B. It appears that they just mix up the groups, first 1 from B, one from H, one from M, one from A, two from B, etc."

75) Coll Ogham – "Coll, c, for a vowel, i.e., group B, group H and group M with no change, and c for group A, i.e., c, cc, ccc, cccc, ccccc."
B, L, F, S, N
H, D, T, C, Q
M, G, NG, STR, R
A – c, O – cc, U – ccc, E – cccc, I – ccccc

87

Ogham: The Secret Language of the Druids

84) Separated Ogham – "The fifth letter is severed." Only the first four letters of each group are used.
   B, L, F, S
   H, D, T, C
   M, G, NG, STR
   A, O, U, E

85) *Ebad*-fashioned Ogham (pronounced 'eb-ath') – "An *Ebad* ✕ between every letter." This is similar to #40 – *Ebad*-Fashioned Ogham, but in this one, the *Ebad* is between the fews. In #40, it is across the few.

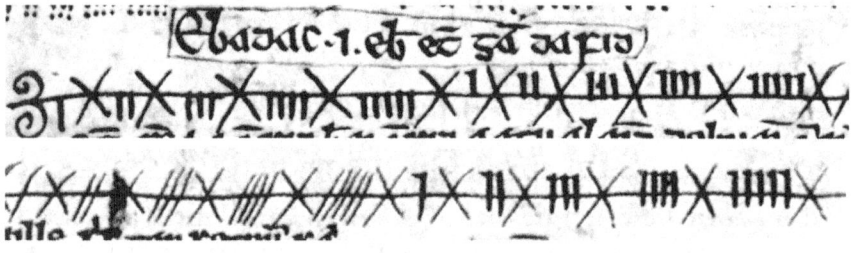

86) Ogham of Fenius – "The letter that touches the letter on its shoulder to be taken off along with it without making use of it." This system adds an extra letter to all fews after the first in each group.
   B - b, L - ll, F - ff, S - ss, N – nn
   H - h, D - dd, T - tt, C - cc, Q - qq
   M - m, G - gg, NG - ngng, STR - strstr, R – rr
   A - a, O - oo, U - uu, E - ee, I – ii

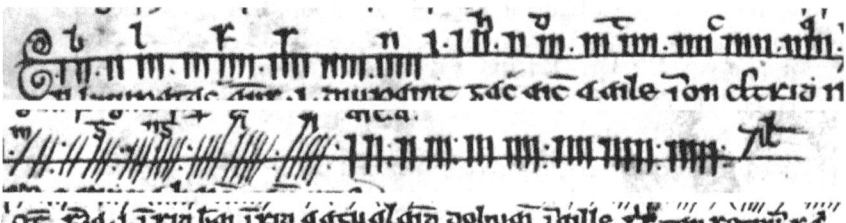

Chapter 3 -Other Oghams from the Scholar's Primer

87) Fraudulent Ogham – Each group's defrauding another of the initial letter. It is the initial letter of the second group, (which ends the first group), *ut est."*

B – l, L – f, F – s, S – n, N – h
H - d, D - t, T - c, C - q, Q – m
M - g, G - ng, NG - str, STR - r, R – a
A - o, O - u, U - e, E - i, I – ea
EA – oi, OI – ui, UI – ia, IA – ae

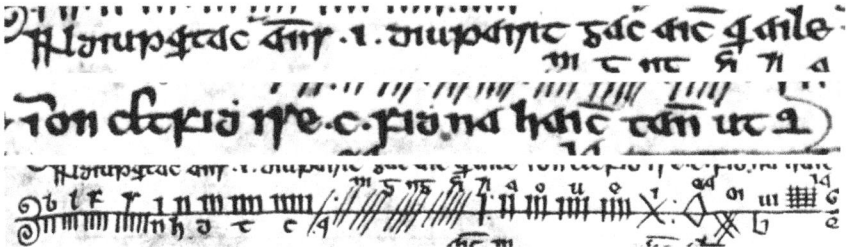

102) Fionn's Window – This ogham is one that has been reproduced in many sources. There are five concentric circles and one symbol from each of the four groups is written on each of the circles. The diphthongs are placed on the 2nd circle in.

The outer circle (#1) has B at the top with the few drawn below (inside) the circle. H is drawn on the right side with the few drawn to the right (outside) of the circle. M is drawn on the bottom of the circle crossing it diagonally (top left and bottom right). A is drawn on the left side with the few crossing the circle.

The 2nd circle has, starting at the top, L, D, G and O with the diphthongs between them as follows: EA is placed between L and D, OI is placed between D and G, UI and IA are placed between G and O and AE is drawn between G and L.

The 3rd circle has, starting at the top, F, T, NG and U.

The 4th circle has, starting at the top, S, C, STR and E.

The 5th circle has, starting at the top, N, Q, R and I.

I will be explaining how we use this ogham for a divination layout in Chapter 4 on divination.

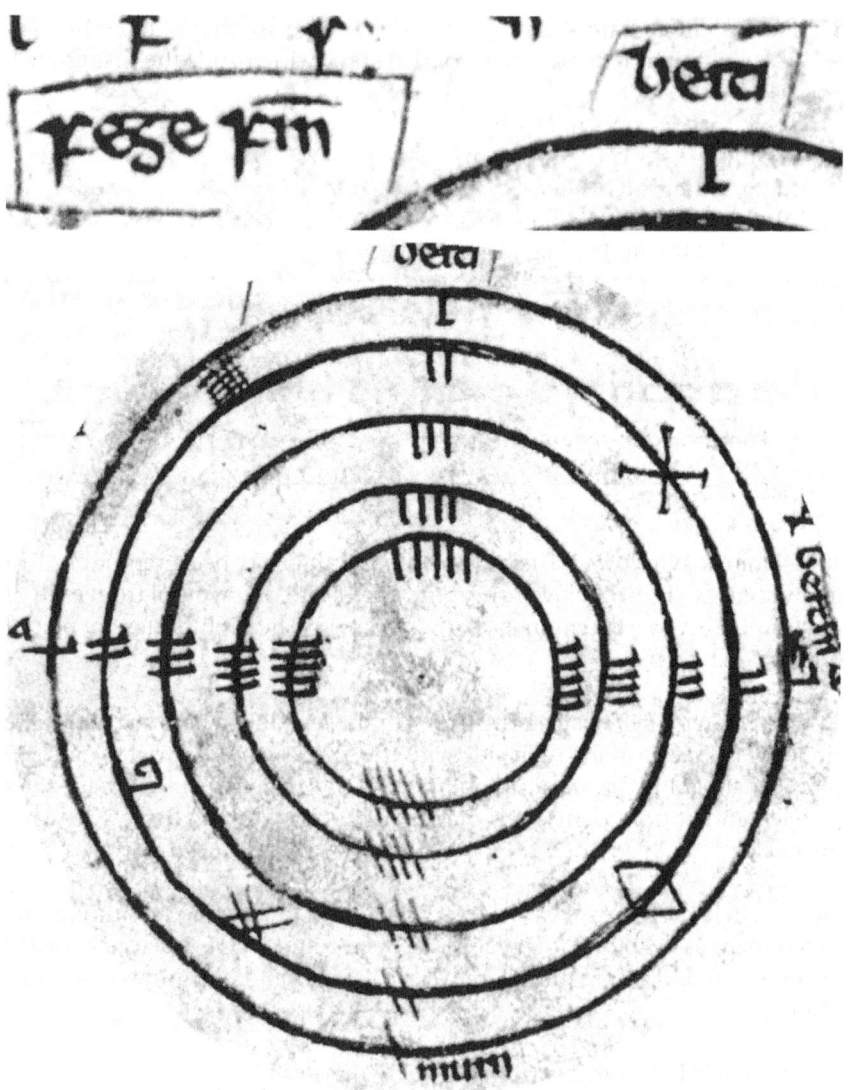

103) Stream Strand of Ferchertne – "Five letters in each thread." This is similar to Fionn's Window #102, but is set up on four squares instead of five circles.

The outer square has B, with the few toward the inside, in the upper left corner, followed by N near the middle of the upper side. L follows this on the right side in the middle, then F on the bottom side. S is on the left side near the top.

Chapter 3 -Other Oghams from the Scholar's Primer

The 2nd square has C at the right side of the top, few toward the outside, followed by H on the top right side. Q follows this on the bottom of the right side. D is on the left of the bottom side and T is on the bottom of the left side.

The 3rd square has NG in the middle of the top, with the diagonal line going from top right to bottom left. STR follows this in the upper part of the right side. M is at the right side of the bottom line, followed by R on the left side of the bottom line. G is on the middle of the left side.

The 4th square has O on the left side of the top line with the few going through the line. U follows this in the middle of the right side. E is in the middle of the bottom side and then A follows on the bottom of the left side. The group is finished with I near the top of the left side.

The diphthongs are written on two lines drawn from the corners of the inside square that cross in the center. UI is on the line going to the upper left corner, IA is on the line going to the upper right corner, OI and EA are both on the line going to the bottom right corner with OI closer to the center. This group is finished with AE drawn on the line going to the bottom left corner. This system is similar to #110 of the same name below.

(See also illustration at the top of the following page)

Ogham: The Secret Language of the Druids

Illustration #2 for Ogham 103

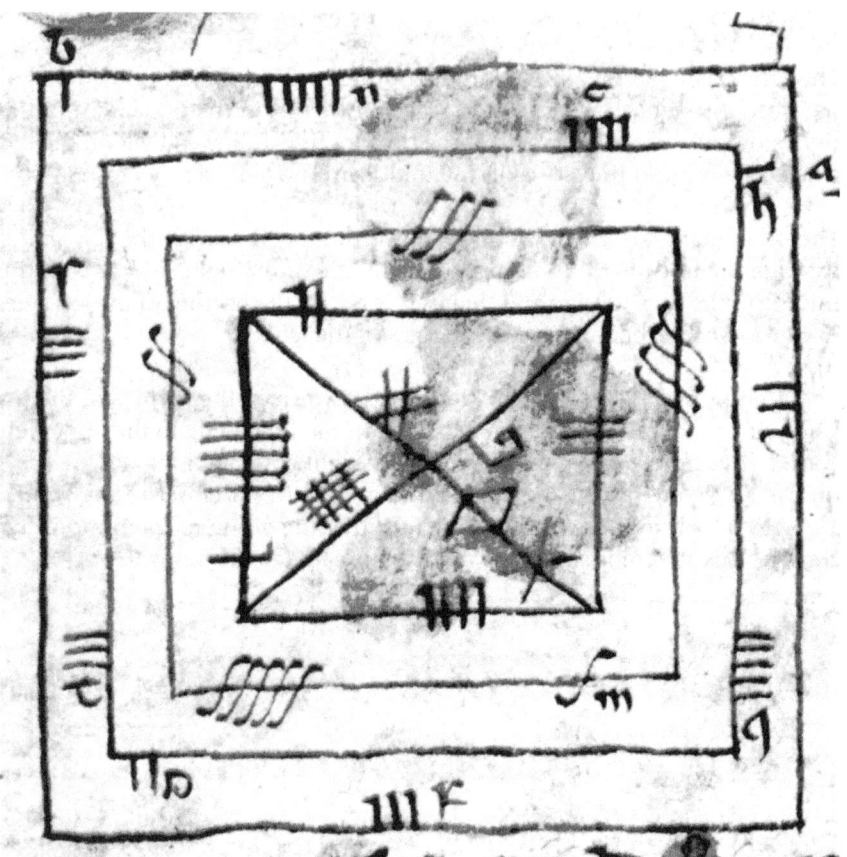

The Mnemonic Lists

2) River Pool Ogham – This system equates the symbols with rivers.
   B – *Barrow*, L – *Lower Shannon*, F – *Foyle*, S – *Shannon*, N – *Nith*
   H – *Othain* (*Fahan*), D – *Dergderg*, T – *Teith*, C – *Catt*, Q – *Cusra*t
   M – *Muinten*, G – *Gavel*, NG – *Graney*, STR – *Sruthair*, R – *Rye*
   A – *Aru*, O – *Eobul*, U – *Uissen*, E – *Erbus*, I – *Indiurnn*

3) Fortress Ogham – This system equates the symbols with fortresses.
   B – *Bruden*, L – *Liffy*, F – *Femen*, S – *Seolae*, N – *Nephin*
   H – *hOcha*, D – *Dinn Rig*, T – *Tara*, C – *Cera*, Q – *Corann*

Chapter 3 -Other Oghams from the Scholar's Primer

M – *Meath*, G – *Gabur*, NG – *nGarman*, STR – *Streulae*, R – *Roigne*
A – *Æ* (Cualand), O – *Odba*, U – *Usney*, E – *Naven*, I - *Islay*

4) Bird Ogham – This system uses birds for the symbols. Question marks show translations that are unsure or not given.

B – *besan* (pheasant?), L – *lachu* (duck), F – *fælinn* (gull), S – *seg* (hawk), N – *næscu* (snipe)

H – *hadaig* (night raven), D – *drone* (wren), T – *truith* (starling), C - ?, Q – *querc* (hen)

M – *mintan* (titmouse), G – *géis* (swan), NG – *ngéigh* (goose), STR – *stinólach* (thrush), R – *rócnat* (small rook)

A – *aidhirccleóg* (lapwing), O – *odoroscrach* (scrat?), U – *uiseóg* (lark), E– *ela* (swan), I – *illait* (eaglet?)

5) Color Ogham – This system uses colors for the symbols.

B – *bán* (white), L – *liath* (grey), F – *flann* (red), S – *sodath* (fine-colored), N – *necht* (clear)

H – *huath* (terrible), D – *dub* (black), T – *temen* (dark grey), C – *cron* (brown), Q – *quiar* (mouse-colored)

M – *mbracht* (variegated), G – *gorm* (blue), NG – *nglas* (green), STR–*sorcha* (bright), R – *ruadh* (red)

A – *alad* (piebald), O – *odhur* (dun), U – *usgdha* (resinous), E – *erc* (red), I – *irfind* (very white)

6) Church Ogham – This system uses the names of Irish churches for the symbols.

B - *Bangor*, L - *Liath*, F - *Ferns*, S - *Saigear*, N – *Noendruim*

H – *hlrard* (Cluain), D – *Durrow*, T – *Terryglass*, C – *Clonmacnois*, Q –*Kildare*

M - *Mugna*, G - ?, NG - ?, STR - *Shrule*, R – *Rahen*, The unknown ones are given as etc.

A - *Armagh*, O - ?, U - ?, E - ?, I - ? The unknown ones are given as etc.

9) Agricultural Ogham – This system uses agricultural implements for the symbols. Question marks show translations that are unsure or not given.

B – *biail* (axe), L – *loman* (rope), F – *fidba* (hedge-bill), S – *srathar* (pack-saddle), N – *nasc* (ring)

H – *huartan* (?), D – *dabach* (cask), T – *tal* (adze), C – *carr* (wagon), Q– *cual* (faggot)

M – *machad* (?), G – *gat* (withe), NG – *ngend* (wedge), STR – *sust* (fl ail), R – *rusc* (basket)

A – *arathar* (plough), O – *ord* (hammer), U – *usca* (heather-brush), E– *epit* (billhook), I – *indeoin* (anvil)

10) King Ogham – This system uses the names of the kings for the letters. We are only given 2 examples, Bran for B and Labride for L, and then it says to give the name of the king that begins with the letter.

21) Saint Ogham – This system uses the names of saints for the symbols.
   B - Brenainn, L - Laisren, F - Finnen, S - Sincheall, N – Neasan
   H - Adamnan, D - Donnan, T - Tighearnach, C - Cronan, Q – Ciaran
   M - Manchan, G - George, NG - nGeminus, STR - Strannan, R – Ruadhan
   A - Aed, O - Oena, U - Ultan, E - Ernen, I – Ita

22) Art Ogham – This system uses different types of work and skills for the symbols.

   B – *bethumnacht* (livelihood), L – *luamnacht* (pilotage), F – *filideacht* (poetry), S – *sairsi* (handicraft), N – *notaireacht* (notary work)

   H – *airchetul* (trisyllacic poetry), D – *druidheacht* (wizardry), T – *tornoracht* (turning), C – *cruitireacht* (harping), Q – *quislenacht* (fluting)

   M – *milaideacht* (soldiering), G – *gaibneacht* (smithwork), NG – *ngibæ* (modeling), STR – *streghuindeacht* (deer-stalking), R – *ronnaireacht* (dispensing)

   A – *airigeacht* (sovereignty), O – *ogmoracht* (harvesting), U – *umaideacht* (brasswork), E – *enaireacht* (fowling), I – *iascaireach* (fishing) or *ibroracht* (yew wood working)

Chapter 3 -Other Oghams from the Scholar's Primer

23) Food Ogham – This system uses common food items for the symbols. All that have come down to us are the terms for B – *bairgen* (bread) and L – *luamnacht* (sweet milk). The rest of the items were so common that everyone would know them.

24) Herb Ogham – This system uses common herbs for the symbols. Unfortunately, we see the same problem here as with the Food Ogham, #23 above. Only the herb for B – *braisech* (kale) has come down to us.

The Gesture Lists

18) Foot Ogham – The fingers of the hand are put across the shinbone. This is one of the gesture langue uses. For the B group they are placed to the right of the leg, for the H group to the left of the leg, for the M group diagonally across the leg and for the A group, straight across the leg. One finger is used for the first letter, 2 for the second, etc.

19) Nose Ogham – This system is very similar to the Foot Ogham, #18 above. However, it uses the bridge of the nose instead of the shinbone of the leg. This is another of the gesture languages.

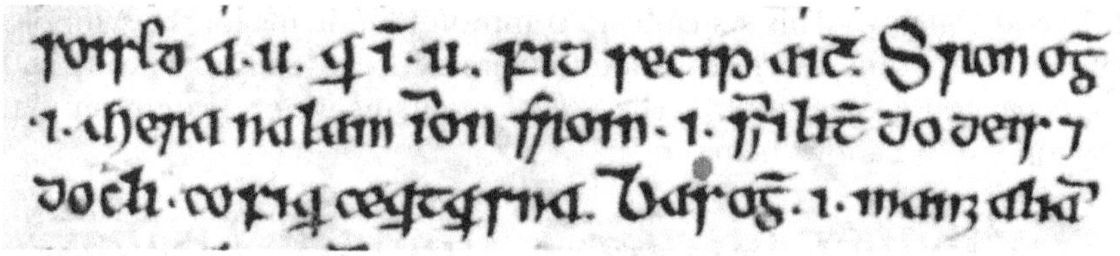

Ogham: The Secret Language of the Druids

[handwritten Irish script]

20) Palm of Hand Ogham – Again, similar to the Foot Ogham, #18 above. This uses the palm of one hand for the straight line. This is another of the gesture languages.

[handwritten Irish script]

The Divination List

17) Boy Ogham – The pregnant woman's name is divided. If she bore a child previously, then the previous child's name is divided. If there is a letter over, i.e. the name has an odd number of letters; then the child will be a boy. If the name has an even number of letters, then the child will be a girl.

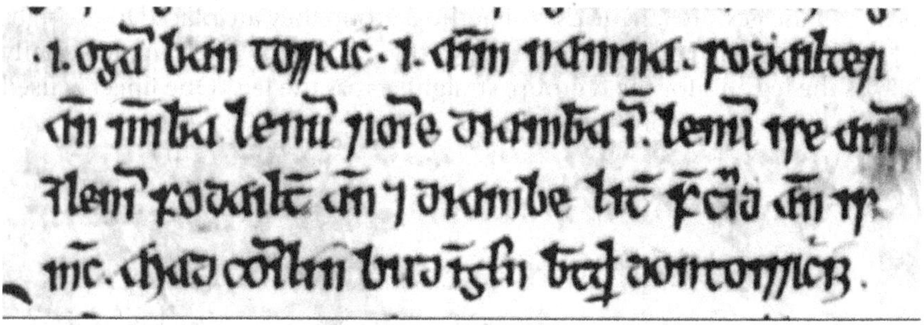

[handwritten Irish script]

The Numbering Lists

1) Sow Ogham – In this system, everything is based on a sow. It is the same as #57 below except that #57 includes different symbols for the Forfeda.

B – white sow, L – grey sow, F – black sow, S – amber sow, N – blue sow

H – white litter with white sow, D – grey, T – black, C – Amber, Q– blue

M – white litter of white sow, G – grey, NG – black, STR – amber, R– blue

A – pig-in-pen of a white sow, O – grey, U – black, E – amber, I– blue

EA – hog-in-pen of a white sow, OI – grey, UI – black, IO – amber, AE– blue

7) Man (Human Being) Ogham – This system uses groups of people for the symbols.

B – 1 man or hero, L – 2 men or heroes, F – 3 men or heroes, S – 4 men or heroes, N – 5 men or heroes

H – 1 women (or nobles or clerics), D – 2 women, T – 3 women, C– 4 women, Q – 5 women

M – 1 youth, G – 2 youths, NG – 3 youths, STR – 4 youths, R – 5 youths

A – 1 boy (or lad), O – 2 boys, U – 3 boys, E – 4 boys, I – 5 boys

8) Woman Ogham – This system uses groups of women for the symbols.

B – 1 heroine, L – 2 heroines, F – 3 heroines, S –4 heroines, N – 5 heroines

H – 1 nun, D – 2 nuns, T – 3 nuns, C – 4 nuns, Q – 5 nuns

M – 1 maiden, G – 2 maidens, NG – 3 maidens, STR – 4 maidens, R– 5 maidens

A – 1 girl, O – 2 girls, U – 3 girls, E – 4 girls, I – 5 girls

11) Water Ogham – This system uses types of water for the symbols.

B – 1 rivulet, L – 2 rivulets, F – 3 rivulets, S – 4 rivulets, N – 5 rivulets

H – 1 weir, D – 2 weirs, T – 3 weirs, C – 4 weirs, Q – 5 weirs

M – 1 river, G – 2 rivers, NG – 3 rivers, STR – 4 rivers, R – 5 rivers

A – 1 well, O – 2 wells, U – 3 wells, E – 4 wells, I – 5 wells

Ogham: The Secret Language of the Druids

12) Dog Ogham – this system uses different types of dogs for the symbols.

B – 1 watch-dog, L – 2 watch-dogs, F – 3 watch-dogs, S – 4 watch-dogs, N – 5 watch-dogs

H – 1 greyhound, D – 2 greyhounds, T – 3 greyhounds, C – 4 greyhounds, Q – 5 greyhounds

M – 1 herd's dog, G – 2 herd's dogs, NG – 3 herd's dogs, STR – 4 herd's dogs, R – 5 herd's dogs

A – 1 lapdog, O – 2 lapdogs, U – 3 lapdogs, E – 4 lapdogs, I – 5 lapdogs

13) Ox Ogham – This system uses different type of cattle for the symbols.

B – 1 bull, L – 2 bulls, F – 3 bulls, S – 4 bulls, N – 5 bulls

H – 1 ox, D – 2 oxen, T – 3 oxen, C – 4 oxen, Q – 5 oxen

M – 1 bullock, G – 2 bullocks, NG – 3 bullocks, STR – 4 bullocks, R – 5 bullocks

A – 1 steer, O – 2 steers, U – 3 steers, E – 4 steers, I – 5 steers

14) Cow Ogham – Another system that uses different types of cows for the symbols.

B – 1 milch cow, L – 2 milch cows, F – 3 milch cows, S – 4 milch cows, N – 5 milch cows

H – 1 stripper, D – 2 strippers, T – 3 strippers, C – 4 strippers, Q – 5 strippers

M – 1 3-year-old heifer, G – 2 3-year-old heifers, NG – 3 3-year-old heifers, STR – 4 3-year-old heifers, R – 5 3-year-old heifers

A – 1 yearling, O – 2 yearlings, U – 3 yearlings, E – 4 yearlings, I – 5 yearlings

Chapter 3 - Other Oghams from the Scholar's Primer

37) Stag Ogham – This system uses types of deer for the symbols.
  B – 1 hart, L – 2 harts, F – 3 harts, S – 4 harts, N – 5 harts
  H – 1 hind, D – 2 hinds, T – 3 hinds, C – 4 hinds, Q – 5 hinds
  M – 1 fawn, G – 2 fawns, NG – 3 fawns, STR – 4 fawns, R – 5 fawns
  A – 1 calf, O – 2 calves, U – 3 calves, E – 4 calves, I – 5 calves

47) Arms Ogham – This system uses types of arms for the symbols.
  B – 1 spear, L – 2 spears, F – 3 spears, S – 4 spears, N – 5 spears
  H – 1 shield, D – 2 shields, T – 3 shields, C – 4 shields, Q – 5 shields
  M – 1 sword, G – 2 swords, NG – 3 swords, STR – 4 swords, R – 5 swords
  A – 1 tusk-hilted sword, O – 2 tusk-hilted swords, U – 3 tusk-hilted swords, E – 4 tusk-hilted swords, I – 5 tusk-hilted swords

57) Sow Ogham – This is exactly the same as the Sow Ogham listed above as number 1 except for the symbols given for the forfeda.

Ogham: The Secret Language of the Druids

B – white sow, L – grey sow, F – black sow, S – amber sow, N – blue sow

H – white litter with white sow, D – grey, T – black, C – Amber, Q – blue

M – white litter of white sow, G – grey, NG – black, STR – amber, R– blue

A – pig-in-pen of a white sow, O – grey, U – black, E – amber, I– blue

EA – hog-in-pen of a white sow, OI – grey, UI – black, IO – amber, AE– blue

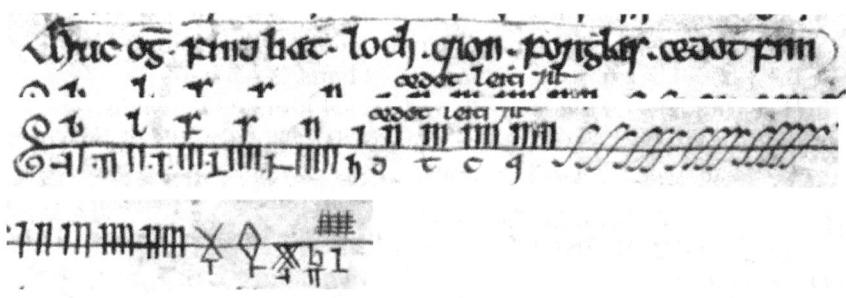

111) Boat Ogham – In this system, types of boats are used for the symbols. Barque for the B group, full rigged ship for the H group, ship for the M group and coracle for the A group. This Ogham is written inside of Ogham #110, which runs along the outside edge.

B – 1 barque, L – 2 barques, F – 3 barques, S – 4 barques, N – 5 barques

H – 1 full-rigged ship, D – 2 full-rigged ships, T – 3 full-rigged ships, C- full-rigged ships, Q – 5 full-rigged ships

M – 1 ship, G – 2 ships, NG – 3 ships, STR – 4 ships, R – 5 ships

A – 1 coracle, O – 2 coracles, U – 3 coracles, E – 4 coracles, I – 5 coracles

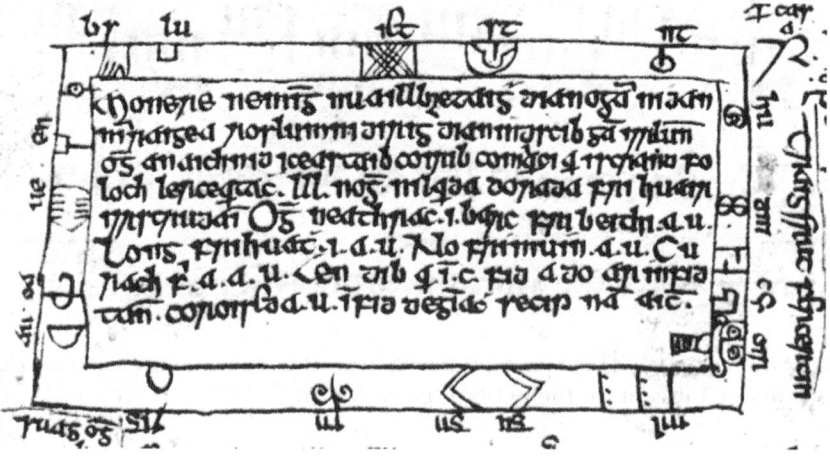

Chapter 3 - Other Oghams from the Scholar's Primer

116) Company Ogham – This system uses companies of people for the symbols. It also includes the diphthongs. It uses priests for the B group, heroines for the H group, Fian for the M group, synods for the A group and saints for the diphthongs.

B – 1 priest, L – 2 priests, F – 3 priests, S – 4 priests, N – 5 priests

H – 1 heroine, D – 2 heroines, T – 3 heroines, C – 4 heroines, Q – 5 heroines

M – 1 Fian, G – 2 Fian's, NG – 3 Fian's, STR – 4 Fian's, R – 5 Fian's

A – 1 synod, O – 2 synods, U – 3 synods, E – 4 synods, I – 5 synods

EA – 1 saint, OI – 2 saints, UI – 3 saints, IA – 4 saints, AE – 5 saints

The Tree Variant Lists

53) Unnamed #4 Ogham – In this variation, the spellings are very close for most of the trees.

B - *beithi*, L - *leam*, F - *fernn*, S - *sail*, N – *nendait*
H - *sge*, D - *dair*, T - *trom*, C - *coll*, Q – *quillenn*
M - *midiu*, G - *gius*, NG - *gilcach*, STR - *saildrong*, R – *rait*
A - *aball*, O - *uinus*, U - *draigin*, E - *ibur*, I – *elend*

Also given for the fifth aicme are *ferus* & *edlend*.

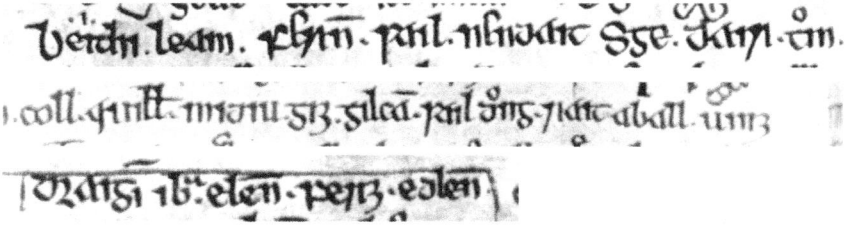

54) Unnamed #5 Ogham - This variation of the tree ogham is interesting in that it lists the diphthongs. It appears to be a manuscript ogham as the M group is written with flourishes on the tips.

B - *bethi*, L - *luis*, F - *fernn*, S - *soil*, N – *nin*
H - *huath*, D - *dur*, T - *tindi*, C - *coll*, Q – *quert*

M - *muin*, G - *gort*, NG - *ngedar*, STR - *straiph*, R – *ruis*
A - *ailm*, O - *onn*, U - *ur*, E - *edadh*, I – *idad*
1st – ea, 2nd – oi, 3rd – ui, 4th – ia, 5th - æ

Finit dona hogmaib – **End of the Oghams**

4
The Use of Oghams in Magic and Divination

Oghams and Magic

In the book *Corpus Inscriptionum Insularum Celticarum* by R. A. S. Macalister, he gives the following description of an artifact found in Cahercommaun and includes the picture shown on the next page:

> "In the excavation of the tenth-century fortified enclosure called Cahercommaun, the report on which has been published in a separate monograph by R.S.A.I, there was found the metacarpal bone of a sheep decorated with zigzag ornament, and bearing what is undoubtedly an Ogham inscription of some cryptical variety. This most likely had a magical purpose—possibly it was one of a series used in divination; compare the four yew rods with Ogham writing upon them, called "the keys of bardism," whereby the Druid Dallan acquired knowledge of a hidden secret, in the tale called *Tochmarc Étáine*. It is useless to try and decipher a short inscription of this kind in any case, it is not more likely than any other "word of power" to mean anything intelligible."[1]

This sheep bone is but one instance of the use of the Oghams in magic. In one version of the story Macalister refers to, *Tochmarc Étáine*, after Étáine has been stolen by Midir, Eochaid Ollathair, also known as the Dagda, searches for a year without finding her.

He has his Druid, Dallán, seek her out. Dallán makes the four rods of yew and inscribes then with Oghams. It is then revealed through his keys of science and his knowledge of the Oghams that Midir is holding Étáine in Brí Léith, his fortress.[2]

Macalister also talks about an amber bead inscribed with Ogham that is

---
1 Macalister, R.A.S. *Corpus Inscriptionum Insularum Celticarum*. Four Courts Press, Dublin, Ireland. 1996 edition. ISBN 1-85182-242-9 Page 56 & 57
2 McManus, page 157.

Ogham: The Secret Language of the Druids

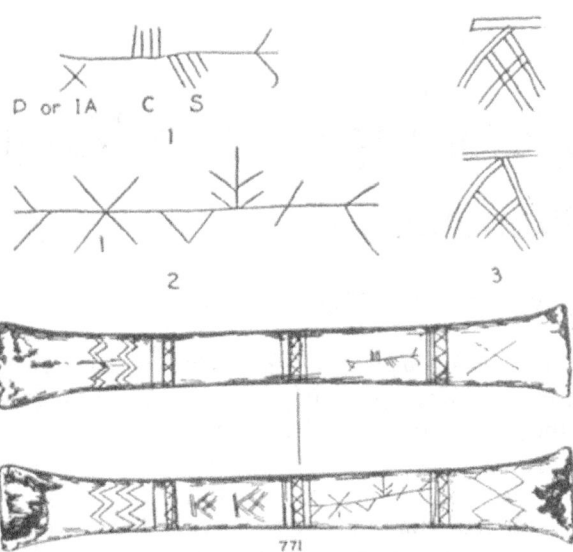

found in the town of Ennis and owned by a family named O'Connor that has been used for curing sore eyes and for easing childbirth.

The translation of the Oghams, if done in the usual fashion, would be ATUC-MLU. This does not mean anything in Irish, so he feels that the Oghams must be from something other than the Tree Ogham and are probably of a magical nature.[3]

A large slab of rock, found in the excavation of an old stone hut on the southern slope of Mount Eagle in County Kerry, bears markings that cannot be interpreted by normal means. These markings bear a slight resemblance to the ones on the amber bead and the slab may have been used for healing purposes, but no actual history of the use of the slab is known.

I believe that the sheep bone, amber bead, and rock are simply three artifacts that have been found but that many more existed than haven't been found yet. Many of the tools used for magic would have been made of, or on wood, such as the yew rods, so we would have to be very lucky to find them now.

There are several examples from the mythological tales of Druids using wands made of hazel branches. I believe that many of these wands were inscribed with Ogham inscriptions to enhance the power of the wands.

---

3 Macalister, page 56 & 57.

Chapter 4 - The Use of Oghams in Magic and Divinations

Why Do We Need to Know Divination?

When we have a problem that needs a magical solution, one effective way to find the best solution is to do a divination. Based on the results, you can plan how you will solve it.

If you are working with your allies from among the Kindreds (the deities, the ancestors, and the nature spirits), receiving feedback from them using divination is also very helpful. This feedback is helpful as you are building your relationships with the Kindreds.

Divination is a skill that grows with practice. If you do a divination each day, say about what will happen during the day, and record the results; you will be surprised at your accuracy rate and how it improves over time.

What Is Divination?

Divination is a way of obtaining knowledge. The knowledge can come from the Kindreds, from the subconscious mind of the person doing the divination, or from some unknown place. Through the ages, there have been many methods used to divine and tell the future. Some of them are listed here.

John Gaule originally published this list in *Mysmantia* in 1652 and I've taken it from *The Encyclopedia of Witchcraft and Demonology* by Rossell Hope Robbins, where it was quoted.[4] I'm including this list because I feel that it is informative about methods that have been used in the past, and that it's something not often seen.

>Aeromancy – or divining by the air.
>Alectryomancy – by cocks or poultry.
>Alphitomancy – by meal, flour or bran.
>Antinopomancy – by the entrails of women and children. *[Not Recommended!]*
>Arithmancy – by numbers.
>Astragalomancy – by dice.
>Axinomancy – by saws.
>Botanomancy – by herbs.
>Capnomancy – by smoke.
>Carromancy – by melting of wax.
>Catoxtromancy – by looking glasses.

---

4 Robbins, Rossell Hope. *The Encyclopedia of Witchcraft and Demonology*. Crown Publishers, Inc., New York, NY. 1959. Page 139.

Cattabomancy – by vessels of brass or other metal.
Cephalonomancy – by boiling of an ass's head.
Chartomancy – by writing in papers.
Chiromancy – by the hands.
Chrystallomancy – by glasses.
Cleromancy – by lots.
Coscinomancy – by sieves.
Crithomancy – by grain or corn.
Dactylomancy – by rings.
Demonomancy – by the suggestion of evil demons or devils.
Gastromancy – by the sound of or signs upon the belly.
Geomancy – by the earth.
Gyromancy – by rounds or circles.
Hydromancy – by water.
Icthyomancy – by fish.
Idolomancy – by idols, images, figures.
Lampadomancy – by candles and lamps.
Lecanomancy – by a basin of water.
Lithomancy – by stones.
Livanomancy – by burning of frankincense.
Logarithmancy – by logarithms.
Macharomancy – by knives or swords.
Oinomancy – by wine.
Omphilomancy – by the navel.
Oniromancy – by dreams.
Onomatomancy – by names.
Onychomancy – by the nails.
Ornithomancy – by birds.
Podomancy – by the feet.
Psychomancy – by men's souls, affections, wills, religious or moral dispositions.
Pyromancy – by fire.
Roadomancy – by the stars.
Sciomancy – by shadows.
Spatalamancy – by skins, bones or excrements.
Stareomancy – or diving by the elements.
Sternomancy – from the breast to the belly.
Sycomancy – by figs.
Theomancy – *pretending* to divine by the revelation of the Spirit and by the Scriptures or Word of God.[5]

---

5 Notice in this definition the use of the word 'pretending,' italics mine. At the time this was originally published, it was believe that the scriptures had been definitively translated and that God wouldn't tell men their future.

Theriomancy – by beasts.
Tuphramancy – by ashes.
Tyromancy – by the coagulation of cheese.
And in one word for all, nagomancy or necromancy, by inspecting, consulting and divining by, with, or from the dead.

How Are Divinations Done?

Divination should be done in the same manner all the time. In a divination, you are allowing your subconscious mind to open up to the message you are receiving. By repeating the same form of actions each time, you let your subconscious know that it is being called upon to do the work.

We know how the ancient Germans practiced divination from the works of the Roman writer, Tacitus, who wrote about the end of the first century CE. In Chapter 10 of his work *Germania*, he writes:

> "To the use of lots and auguries, they are addicted beyond all other nations. Their method of divining by lots is exceedingly simple. From a tree which bears fruit they cut a twig, and divide it into two small pieces. These they distinguish by so many several marks, and throw them at random and without order upon a white garment. Then the Priest of the community, if for the public the lots are consulted, or the father of a family about a private concern, after he has solemnly invoked the Gods, with eyes lifted up to heaven, takes up every piece thrice, and having done thus forms a judgment according to the marks before made. If the chances have proved forbidding, they are no more consulted upon the same affair during the same day: even when they are inviting, yet, for confirmation, the faith of auguries too is tried. Yea, here also is the known practice of divining events from the voices and flight of birds.
>
> But to this nation it is peculiar, to learn presages and admonitions divine from horses also. These are nourished by the State in the same sacred woods and groves, all milk-white and employed in no earthly labor. These yoked in the holy chariot, are accompanied by the Priest and the King, or the Chief of the Community, who both carefully observe his actions and neighing. Nor in any sort of augury is more faith and assurance reposed, not by the populace only, but even by the nobles, even by the Priests.

> These account themselves the ministers of the Gods, and the horses privy to their will. They have likewise another method of divination, whence to learn the issue of great and mighty wars. From the nation with whom they are at war they contrive, it avails not how, to gain a captive: him they engage in combat with one selected from amongst themselves, each armed after the manner of his country, and according as the victory falls to this or to the other, gather a presage of the whole."[6]

From this, we see that lots (no one is sure if Tacitus was talking about Runes or Oghams in this paragraph) were made of wood from fruit trees. Fruit trees also included nut trees, so there is a wide range of material that could be used to make them from. We also see that divinations were done after turning the face up to the Gods and praying for a good omen. All in all, there is quite a bit of information in this one section to show us the mechanics of doing the divination.

When I'm doing a divination, I start by spreading a white rabbit's fur on the table or ground where I'm doing the divination. White is a traditional color for a divining cloth and when I passed the rabbit fur in a shop in New Mexico, it called out to me and I had to get it.

Next I hold my bag of Oghams, my primary divination tool, up in the air and say a short prayer that my reading will be true. I shake the bag while saying the prayer to allow the 'proper' Oghams to come to the top. I then put my hand in and pick the first three disks I touch, unless something tells me to dig deeper. That does sometimes happen. This is why it is important to be 'open' at this time.

With the three Oghams drawn, I lay them out and read them from left to right. My usual method is the one on the left is from the Nature Spirits, the center one is from the Ancestors, and the one on the right is from the Shining Ones. I may also use Past, Present, and Future if needed.

Several other layouts and methods work well with the Oghams. One interesting one uses Fionn's Window (Other Ogham #102). For this method, a *bodhran*, an Irish hoop drum, is used. The cross sticks on the back of the drum are used to divide the circle of the drum into four quadrants. Each quadrant represents the quadrants in Fionn's Window. Small stones or markers can be used for the divination. Where they land in the drum is the corresponding letter/tree from Fionn's Window.

---

6 Halsall, Paul. http://www.fordham.edu/halsall/source/ tacitus1.html. Medieval Sourcebook, entry on Tacitus, and text of Germania.

Chapter 4 - The Use of Oghams in Magic and Divinations

Another method is to lay the disks out in the form of an equal-armed cross. This method used a total of nine disks. The center disk is you and the tree that represents you. The two disks above the center are the problems above you, problems that you need to be aware of but have little control over. The two disks below the center are the things below you, things that you do have control over. The two disks to the left of the center are things behind you; problems or influences that you've already handled or are that are in your past. The two disks to the right of the center are problems still ahead of you, or things of which you need to be aware.

A new divination method for the oghams that I've developed this year is called the *cúige* [pronounced *ku-ga* and meaning portions, fifths or provinces] or 'Provinces of Ireland'. This method is based on the diagram shown below. This diagram is placed on the bottom of a box and then all of the ogham disks are tossed into the air so that they fall at random into the five sections.

The divination meanings derive first, from where the disk falls, and then the

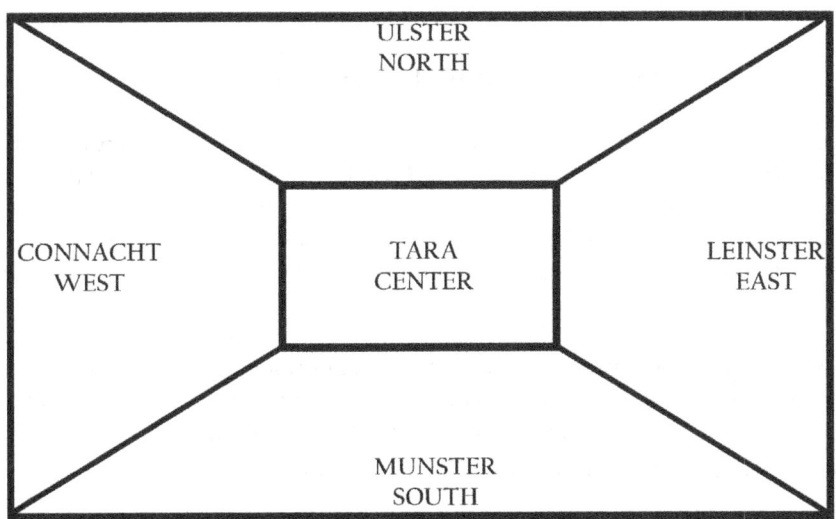

usual meaning given to the tree associated with the few. The meanings for the sectors are:

> Tara – the Center. In Tara is where you find the things that matter the most to you and that mean the most to you. This is also the position of the present, the here and now.
> • Connacht – the West. In Connacht is where you find your

emotional issues, those that affect you on an instinctive level. This is also the position of the past, what you've put behind you.
- Ulster – the North. In Ulster is where you reflect on what is learned and where you find what you need to learn. This is also the position of withdrawal and introspection.
- Leinster – the East. In Leinster is where you find your logical issues, those that you need to 'work' through to resolve. This is also the position of the future, those things that lie ahead.
- Munster – the South. In Munster is where you find you the issue that burn within you, those you feel strongest about. This is also the position of active work on problems.

This system has the advantage of being able to give you a very detailed reading. In this system, it is important that the client expresses the question in a general, rather than specific manner. This allows the fews to give the details, instead of the client.

General Guidelines for Divination Tools

I have found that divination tools, be they Ogham discs, runes, crystal ball, tarot cards, or whatever, all work best if you keep them in a special darkened place. For the ogham discs, along with runes and tarot cards, a special bag works well. When you first get the tools, it helps to develop a connection with them by sleeping with them either under your mattress or near your bed.

These special tools work best if they are used on a regular basis. If you've put your Oghams away for say six months, do not expect to be able to pick them up and get accurate answers right away! The interplay and connections between you and them need to be kept up.

Ways to improve your Divination

The best way, by far, to improve your divination skill is practice, practice, practice! The more often you use your tools, the closer the connection between you and them grows and the better able you are to 'understand' what they are trying to show you. Many people firmly believe in keeping a close physical connection to their tools, even when they are not being used. This can be done by carrying the tools with you at all times or by sleeping with the tools in close proximity.

Another way to improve your skill is by reading and studying about your favorite method. If you like runes, there are dozens of good books by respected scholars on the origins and uses of the runes in ancient time. The more you learn about them, the greater the pool of 'useful information bits' that your subconscious will tap into during a reading. You do not have to try and consciously memorize all the material; having read it once, you will be able to tap into it when you need to.

A third way to improve your divination skill is by meditating with you tools. Try to spend time at least once a week where your mediation involves just your tools. One way to do this is by spreading them all out before you on a table. With your eyes closed, allow your hand to slowly move over them, noting any 'odd' or 'different' perceptions you may feel. Do not hesitate to let yourself linger over one or two if it feels right. This isn't an exercise to memorize the tools or to learn the different symbols; it is simply to allow your subconscious to tap into them better. The visual clues we receive from the tools are important, but what our subconscious 'feels' from them is just as important.

Ethics for the Diviner

These are guidelines that I feel all people who practice divination should abide by. These guidelines that been put together with help from the Ethics Policies from the Seer's Guilds of Muin Mound Grove, ADF and Shining Lakes Grove, ADF along with the Ethics Policy of the ADF Seer's Guild.[7]

1. A diviner shall hold faithful to the idea that anything talked about during a session with a client will remain confidential, except in extreme extenuating circumstances, such as those that would cause injury to the client or other persons. In that case, the diviner will notify the proper personnel to prevent the injuries. For example, if a client revealed to you that they were planning to kill themselves or others, you should do what you can to try to talk them out of it, as well as notify the police after the client has left.

2. A diviner shall not use their position of trust to exert any undue influence over the client. This will include but not

---

[7] The National Seer's Guild Ethics Policy, those from Shining Lakes Grove, ADF, and of Muin Mound Grove, ADF are no longer available online.

be limited to sexual exploitation, personal advancement or financial gain.

3. A diviner shall refrain from interfering in their clients' life choices, unless the client is in immediate danger (See #1 above). The diviner advises, not pressures.

4. No diviner shall misrepresent his or her abilities or capabilities to a client.

5. A diviner should avoid consulting with a client if it would present a conflict of interest.

5
The Battle of the Trees

A Warning about Robert Graves

I feel that I should write this section because so many people get their first impression of the Oghams from material that is reprinted from *The White Goddess* by Robert Graves.

Graves was a very good poet, but he really was not an expert in Celtic material. His main field of study was poetry and Greek history. In those fields, he was very good and deserves respect.

One place where this lack of Celtic scholarship really shows is in the "Celtic Tree Calendar." In this, he associates thirteen of the trees from the Oghams with months of the year. He outlines this on pages 165–188 in *The White Goddess*.

This was really made up strictly by him, and has no historical basis. This "calendar" has been very heavily re-printed, and many people believe it is the calendar the Druids used, which is completely not true! It only dates back to the 1940's.

At the start of his "re-telling" of the *Câd Goddeu*, the Battle of the Trees, he specifically tells the readers that he did not understand Welsh and was not a Welsh scholar. He says,

> "Here I must apologize for my temerity in writing on a subject which is not really my own. I am not a Welshman, except an honorary one through eating a leek on St. David's Day while serving with the Royal Welch Fusiliers and, though I have lived in Wales for some years, off and on, have no command even of modern Welsh; and I am not a mediaeval historian."[1]

He then proceeded to deconstruct the translation of the poem, **not the original** mind you, because he could not understand its meaning. He redid it so that it made sense to him.

---

1 Graves, pages 29–30.

It didn't matter to him that many people had been able to understand what Taliesin, the original author of the poem, had meant through the years; because he couldn't understand it, the poem had to be wrong, so he had to re-write it.

It is unfortunate that it is this rewriting that gets reprinted all the time and many people today do not understand that it is not the original, but simply a 1940s retelling.

There have been many translations of the "Battle of the Trees." I've included three here so that you can see the differences for yourself and, in the case of the re-working by Graves, see the changes he made so that he could "understand" it and compare Graves' version of the *Câd Goddeu* with genuinely scholarly translations.

In order, there is the translation by D. W. Nash quoted by Robert Graves in *The White Goddess*, and then Grave's own re-working, and finally, the translation by Patrick K. Ford from *The Mabinogi and Other Medieval Welsh Tales*. Modern scholars consider the last to be the best translation.

CÂD GODDEU
The Battle of the Trees
Translation by D. W. Nash[1]

1	"I have been in many shapes, Before I attained a congenial form. I have been a narrow blade of a sword. (I will believe it when it appears.)
5	I have been a drop in the air. I have been a shining Star. I have been a word in a book. I have been a book originally. I have been a light in a lantern.
10	A year and a half. I have been a bridge for passing over Threescore rivers. I have journeyed as an eagle. I have been a boat on the sea.
15	I have been a director in battle. I have been the string of a child's swaddling clout. I have been a sword in the hand. I have been a shield in the fight. I have been the string of a harp,

---
[1] Quoted from: Graves, Robert. *The White Goddess.* Farrar, Straus and Giroux, 19 Union Square West, NY, NY 10003. 1982. ISBN – 374504938. Pages 30-36.

Chapter 5- The Battle of the Trees

20　　Enchanted for a year In the foam of water. I have been a poker in the fire. I have been a tree in a covert. There is nothing in which I have not been.

25　　I have fought, though small, In the Battle of Goddeu Brig, Before the Ruler of Britain, Abounding in fleets. Indifferent bards pretend,

30　　They pretend a monstrous beast, With a hundred heads, And a grievous combat At the root of the tongue. And another fight there is

35　　At the back of the head. A toad having on his thighs A hundred claws, A spotted crested snake, For punishing in their flesh

40　　A hundred souls on account of their sins. I was in Caer Fefynedd, Thither were hastening grasses and trees. Wayfarers perceive them, Warriors are astonished

45　　At a renewal of the conflicts Such as Gwydion made. There is calling on Heaven, And on Christ that he would effect Their deliverance,

50　　The all-powerful Lord. If the Lord had answered, Through charms and magic skill, Assume the forms of the principal trees, With you in array

55　　Restrain the people, The Druids' Alphabet Inexperienced in battle. When the trees were enchanted There was hope for the trees, That they should frustrate the intention

60　　Of the surrounding fires.... Better are three in unison, And enjoying themselves in, a circle, And one of them relating The story of the deluge,

65　　And of the cross of Christ, And of the Day of Judgement near at hand. The alder-trees in the first line, They made the commencement. Willow and quicken tree,

70　　They were slow in their array. The plum is a tree Not beloved of men; The medlar of a like nature, Over coming severe toil.

75　　The bean bearing in its shade And army of phantoms. The raspberry makes Not the best of food. In shelter live,

80　　The privet and the woodbine, And the ivy in its season. Great is the gorse in battle. The cherry-tree had been reproached. The birch, though very magnanimous,

85   Was late in arraying himself; It was not through cowardice, But on account of his great size. The appearance of the ... Is that of a foreigner and a savage.

90   The pine-tree in the court, Strong in battle, By me greatly exalted In the presence of kings, The elm-trees are his subjects.

95   He turns not aside the measure of a foot, But strikes right in the middle, And at the farthest end. The hazel is the judge, His berries are thy dowry.

100 The privet is blessed. Strong chiefs in war And the ... and the mulberry. Prosperous the beech-tree. The holly dark green,

105 He was very courageous: Defended with spikes on every side, Wounding the hands. The long-enduring poplars Very much broken in fight.

110 The plundered fern; The brooms with their offspring: The furze was not well behaved Until he was tamed The heath was giving consolation,

115 Comforting the people – The black cherry-tree was pursuing. The oak-tree swiftly moving, Before him tremble heaven and earth, Stout doorkeeper against the foe

120 Is his name in all lands. The corn-cockle bound together, Was given to be burnt. Others were rejected On account of the holes made

125 By great violence In the field of battle. Very wrathful the ... Cruel the gloomy ash. Bashful the chestnut-tree,

130 Retreating from happiness. There shall be a black darkness, There shall be a shaking of the mountain, There shall be a purifying furnace, There shall first be a great wave,

135 And when the shout shall be heard, Putting forth new leaves are the tops of the beech, Changing form and beingrenewed from a withered state; Entangled are the tops of the oak. From the Gorchan of Maelderw.

140 Smiling at the side of the rock (Was) the pear-tree not of an ardent nature. Neither of mother or father, When I was made, Was my blood or body;

145 Of nine kinds of faculties, Of fruit of fruits, Of fruit God made me, Of the blossom of the mountain primrose, Of the buds of trees and shrubs,

Chapter 5- The Battle of the Trees

150 Of earth of earthly kind. When I was made Of the blossoms of the nettle, Of the water of the ninth wave, I was spellbound by Math

155 Before I became immortal. I was spell-bound by Gwydion, Great enchanter of the Britons, Of Eurys, of Eurwn, Of Euron, of Medron,

160 In myriads of secrets, I am as learned as Math.... I know about the Emperor When he was half burnt. I know the star-knowledge

165 Of stars before the earth (was made), Whence I was born, How many worlds there are. It is the custom of accomplished bards To recite the praise of their country.

170 I have played in Lloughor, I have slept in purple. Was I not in the enclosure With Dylan Ail Mor, On a couch in the centre

175 Between the two knees of the prince Upon two blunt spears? When from heaven came The torrents into the deep, Rushing with violent impulse.

180 (I know) four-score songs, For administering to their pleasure. There is neither old nor young, Except me as to their poems, Any other singer who knows the whole of the nine hundred

185 Which are known to me, Concerning the blood-spotted sword. Honour is my guide. Profitable learning is from the Lord. (I know) of the slaying of the boar,

190 Its appearing, its disappearing, Its knowledge of languages. (I know) the light whose name is Splendour, And the number of the ruling lights That scatter rays of fire

195 High above the deep. I have been a spotted snake upon a hill; I have been a viper in a lake; I have been an evil star formerly. I have been a weight in a mill. (?)

200 My cassock is red all over. I prophesy no evil. Four score puffs of smoke To every one I who will carry them away: And a million of angels,

205 On the point of my knife. Handsome is the yellow horse, But a hundred times better Is my cream-coloured one, Swift as the sea-mew,

210 Which cannot pass me Between the sea and the shore. Am I not pre-eminent in the field of blood? I have a hundred shares of

215 the spoil. My wreath is of red jewels, Of gold is the border of my shield. There has not been born one so good as I, Or ever known, Except Goronwy, From the dales of Edrywy.

220 Long and white are my fingers, It is long since I was a herdsman. I travelled over the earth Before I became a learned person. I have travelled, I have made a circuit,

225 I have slept in a hundred islands; I have dwelt in a hundred cities. Learned Druids, Prophesy ye of Arthur? Or is it me they celebrate,

230 And the Crucifixion of Christ, And the Day of Judgement near at hand, And one relating The history of the Deluge? With a golden jewel set in gold

235 I am enriched; And I am indulging in pleasure Out of the oppressive toil of the goldsmith."

CÂD GODDEU
The Battle of the Trees
Re-working by Robert Graves[1]

"The tops of the beech tree
Have sprouted of late,
Are changed and renewed
From their withered state.

When the beech prospers,
Though spells and litanies
The oak tops entangle,
There is hope for trees.

I have plundered the fern,
Through all secrets I spy,
Old Math ap Mathonwy
Knew no more than I.

---

[1] Quoted from: Graves, Robert. *The White Goddess*. Farrar, Straus and Giroux, 19 Union Square West, NY, NY 10003. 1982. ISBN – 374504938. Pages 30-36.

Chapter 5- The Battle of the Trees

For with nine sorts of faculty
God has gifted me,
I am fruit of fruits gathered
From nine sorts of tree—

Plum, quince, whortle, mulberry,
Raspberry, pear,
Black cherry and white,
With the sorb in me share.

From my seat at Fefynedd,
A city that is strong,
I watched the trees and green things
Hastening along.

Retreating from happiness
They would fain be set
In forms of the chief letters
Of the alphabet.

Wayfarers wandered,
Warriors were dismayed
At renewal of conflicts
Such as Gwydion made;

Under the tongue root
A fight most dread,
And another raging,
Behind, in the head.

The alders in the front line
Began the affray.
Willow and rowan-tree
Were tardy in array.

The holly, dark green,
Made a resolute stand;
He is armed with many spear-points
Wounding the hand.

With foot-beat of the swift oak
Heaven and earth rung;
'Stout Guardian of the Door,'

His name in every tongue.

Great was the gorse in battle,
And the ivy at his prime;
The hazel was arbiter
At this charmed time.

Uncouth and savage was the fir,
Cruel the ash tree—
Turns not aside a foot-breadth,
Straight at the heart runs he.

The birch, though very noble,
Armed himself but late:
A sign not of cowardice
But of high estate.

The heath gave consolation
To the toil-spent folk,
The long-enduring poplars
In battle much broke.

Some of them were cast away
On the field of fight
Because of holes torn in them
By the enemy's might.

Very wrathful was the vine
Whose henchmen are the elms;
I exalt him mightily
To rulers of realms.

Strong chieftains were the blackthorn
With his ill fruit,
The unbeloved whitethorn
Who wears the same suit.

The swift-pursuing reed,
The broom with his brood,
And the furze but ill-behaved
Until he is subdued.

The dower-scattering yew
Stood glum at the fight's fringe,

With the elder slow to burn
Amid fires that singe.

And the blessed wild apple
Laughing in pride
From the Gorchan of Maeldrew,
By the rock side.

In shelter linger
Privet and woodbine,
Inexperienced in warfare,
And the courtly pine.

But I, although slighted
Because I was not big,
Fought, trees, in your array
On the field of Goddeu Brig."

CÂD GODDEU
The Battle of the Trees
Translation by Patrick K. Ford

1   "I was in many shapes before I was released: I was a slender, enchanted sword—I believe that it was done. I was raindrops in the air, I was stars' beam; I was a word in letters, I was a book in origin;

5   I was lanterns of light for a year and a half; I was a bridge that stretched over sixty estuaries; I was a path, I was an eagle, I was a coracle in seas; I was a bubble in beer, I was a drop in a shower; I was a sword in hand, I was a shield in battle.

10 I was a string in a harp enchanted nine years, in the water as foam; I was a spark in fire, I was wood in a bonfire; I am not one who does not sing; I have sung since I was small I sang in the army of the trees' branches before the ruler of Britain. I wounded swift horses, destroyed powerful fleets;

15 I wounded a great scaly animal: a hundred heads on him And a fierce host beneath the base of his tongue, And another host is on his necks. A black, forked toad:

a hundred claws on him. An enchanted, crested snake in whose skin a hundred souls are punished

20 I was in Caer Nefenhir where grass and trees attacked, Poets sang, warriors rushed forth. Gwydion raised his staff of enchantment, Called upon the Lord, upon Christ, making pleas So that he, the Lord who had made him, might deliver him.

25 The Lord replied in language and in the land: 'Transform stalwart trees into armies with him and obstruct Peblig the powerful from giving battle.' When the trees were enchanted, in the hope of our purpose, They hewed down trees with ...

30 Three chieftains fell in grievous days' battles. A maiden uttered a bitter sigh, grief broke forth; Foremost in lineage, pre-eminent maiden. Life and wakefulness Gain us no vantage in Mellun: men's blood up to our thighs. The three greatest upheavals that have happened in the world;

35 And one comes to pass in the story of the flood, And Christ's crucifying, and then Doomsday. Alder, pre-eminent in lineage, attacked in the beginning; Willow and rowan were late to the army; Thorny plum was greedy for slaughter;

40 Powerful dogwood, resisting prince; Rose-trees went against a host in wrath; Raspberry bushes performed, did not make an enclosure For the protection of life ... and honeysuckle And ivy for its beauty; sea gorse for terror;

45 Cherries mocked; birch for high-mindedness—it was late that it armed, Not because of cowardice, but because of greatness. Goldenrod held a shape, foreigners over foreign waters; Fir trees to the fore, ruler in battles; Ash performed excellently before monarchs;

50 Elm because of its ferocity did not budge a foot: It would strike in the middle, on the flanks, and in the end. Hazel wood was deemed arms for the tumult; Happy the privet, bull of battle, lord of the world ... fir trees prospered;

55	Holly turned green, it was in battle; Fine hawthorn delivered pain; Attacking vines attacked in battle; Destructive fern; broom before the host Were plowed under. Gorse was not lucky,
60	But despite that it was turned into an army, fine fighting heather Was changed into a host, pursuer of men. Swift and mighty oak: before him trembled heaven and earth; Fierce enemy of warriors, his name in wax tablets. ... tree gave terror in combat;
65	He used to oppose, he opposed others from a hole; Pear worked oppression in the battlefield, Fearful drawing up of a flood of noble trees. Chestnut, shame of the prince of fir trees. Jet is black, mountains are rounded, trees are sharp;
70	Great seas are swifter since I heard the scream. Tips of birch sprouted for us, immutable energy; Tips of oak stained for us from Gwarchan Maelderw Laughing from the hillside, a lord not ... Not from a mother and father was I made;
75	As for creation, I was created from nine forms of elements: From the fruit of fruits, from the fruit of God at the beginning; From primroses and flowers of the hill, from the blooms of woods and trees; From the essence of soils was I made, From the bloom of nettles, from water of the ninth wave.
80	Math enchanted me before I was mobile; Gwydion created me, great magic from the staff of enchantment; From Eurwys and Euron, from Euron and Modron, From five fifties of magicians and teachers like Math was I produced. The lord produced me when he was quite inflamed;
85	The magician of magicians created me before the world— When I had existence, there was expanse to the world. Fair bard! Our custom is profit; I can put in song what the tongue can utter. I passed time at dawn, I slept in purple; I was in the rampart with Dylan Eil Mor,
90	In a cloak in the middle between kings, In two lusty spears that came from heaven; In Annwfn they will sharpen in the battle to which they will come; Four-

score hundred I pierced because of their lust— They are neither older nor younger than me in their passion.

95 The passion of a hundred men is needed by each, I had that of nine hundred. In an enchanted sword, renowned blood flowing in me from a lord from his place of concealment; from a drop was the warrior killed. Peoples were made, remade, and made again.

100 The brilliant one his name, the strong hand; like lightning he governed the host. They scattered in sparks from the tame one on high. I was a snake enchanted in a hill, I was a viper in a lake; I was a star with a shaft; I was this huntingshaft. Not badly shall I prepare my cloak and cup.

105 Four twenties of smoke will come upon each. Five fifties of bonds-maids the value of my knife; Six yellowish-brown horses—a hundred times is better; My pale-yellow horse is swift as a seagull; I myself am not feeble between sea and shore.

110 I shall cause a field of blood, on it a hundred warriors; Scaly and red my shield, gold is my shield-ring. There was not born in Adwy anyone who attacked me Except Goronwy from Doleu Edrywy. Long and white are my fingers; long have I not been a shepherd;

115 I lived as a warrior before I was a man of letters; I wandered, I encircled, I slept in a hundred islands, I dwelt in a hundred forts. Druids, wise one, prophesy to Arthur; There is what is before, they perceive what has been. And one occurs in the story of the flood

120 And Christ's crucifying and then Doomsday. Golden goldskinned, I shall deck myself in riches, And I shall be in luxury because of the prophecy of Virgil.

Appendix 1

A Quick Refference - The Tree Ogham

Symbol	Aicme - Few	Tree	Name	Other Names	Letter	Meaning
┬	1 - 1	Birch	Beith	Beth [1,2] Beithe [3] Beith [4]	B	New Beginnings
┬┬	1 - 2	Rowan	Luis		L	Protection & control of senses
┬┬┬	1 - 3	Alder	Fern		F	Guidance, associated with Bran
┬┬┬┬	1 - 4	Willow	Sail	Saille [1,2]	S	Mysteries and water related subjects, feminine attributes
┬┬┬┬┬	1 - 5	Ash	Nion	Nin [3] Nuin [4]	N	Ancient knowledge, the weaver's beam
┴	2 - 1	Hawthorn	Uath	Huath [2,3] Huath [4]	H	Counseling protection and cleansing
┴┴	2 - 2	Oak	Dair	Duir [1,2,3]	D	Wisdom and Strength
┴┴┴	2 - 3	Holly	Tinne		T	Justice & balance
┴┴┴┴	2 - 4	Hazel	Coll		C	Wisdom & intuition
┴┴┴┴┴	2 - 5	Apple	Ceirt	Quert [1,2] Queirt [3] Cert [4]	Q	The Otherworld & choice
╱	3 - 1	Vine	Muin		M	Prophecy & inhibition or lack of
╱╱	3 - 2	Ivy	Gort		G	Search for yourself & inner wisdom
╱╱╱	3 - 3	Broom	nGéadal	nGetal [1,2,3]	NG or GG	Working & tools
╱╱╱╱	3 - 4	Blackthorn	Straif	Straiph [3]	ST, STR, Z	Trouble & negativity

125

Symbol	Aicme - Few	Tree	Name	Other Names	Letter	Meaning
⊞	3 - 5	Elder	Ruis		R	Entrance to the Otherworld & the Fair Folk
┼₅	4 - 1	Silver Fir	Ailm	Ailim[2]	A	Far seeing & knowing the future
╫	4 - 2	Gorse	Onn		O	Collecting things to you
╬	4 - 3	Heather	Úr	Ura[1] Ur[2,3]	U	Healing & homelands
⧻	4 - 4	Aspen	Eadhadh	Eadha[1,2] Edad[3,4]	E	Communication
⧼	4 - 5	Yew	Iodhadh	Idho[1] Iodho[2] Idad[3]	I	Death & rebirth
✳	5 - 1*	White Poplar	Éabhadh	Ebad[3] Ébad[4]	EA	Buoyancy & floating above problems
4	5 - 2	Spindle	Ór	Oir[3]	OI	Community, working within the home
⌇₆	5 - 3	Honey-suckle	Uilleann	Uileand[3] Uilen[4]	UI	Drawing things together and binding
⋈₇	5 - 4	Gooseberry	Ifín	Iphin[3]	IO	The Kindreds, especially of Nature
☰₈	5 - 5	Witch-hazel	Eamhan-choll	Phagos[3] Eman-choll[4]	AE	Magic and hidden knowledge
∇∇	6 - 1"	Norway Maple	Mailp			Modifier for the land.
◇◇	6 - 2	Rush (Reed)	Brobh			Modifier for the sea.
△△△	6 - 3	Bird Cherry	Craobh Fhiod-hag			Modifier for the sky.
≻			Eite	Saighead[4]		Feather or arrow – used to show direction to be read.
			Spás	Bearna[4]		Space – also seen as •or :

Appendix 1 - Quick Reference - The Tree Ogham

Key to the Notations

* - The 5th aicme, also known as the diphthongs, are not used in some divination systems because they were not part of the original Oghams. They were added at a later time. Most systems do not associate trees with them, but in my system, I have.

** - I have added the 6th aicme in my system as well, to be used as modifiers. This is not normally found in the Ogham systems.

1 As used by Robert Graves in *The White Goddess*.

2 As used by Nigel Pennick in *The Celtic Oracle*.

3 As used by Eldred Thorsson – AKA Stephen Flowers.

4 As used by Michael Everson.

5 The 4th aicme, or vowels, are sometimes shown as dots on the line as well as the full line across.

6 This figure is drawn facing both to the left and to the right.

7 This figure is shown drawn with from 2 to 4 cross lines.

8 This figure is shown drawn both above and below the line.

Appendix 2

Making Your Own Ogham Discs

The format I use on the front of these disks is Irish name, pronunciation, symbol, English name, aicme – few, and class. On the back, I have the aicme – few and a one word "reminder" in case nothing comes through.

The first step in this part of the process, which is a very important one, is choosing which disk will represent each few. Spread all the disks out on a table in front of you and place the picture of the entire ogham set above them. Start by concentrating your focus on the picture of the few for the letter 'B'. While looking at that, and *NOT* at the disks, run your hand over the disks until one "feels" right for this letter. Pick that one up, and place the numbers 1-1 lightly on it with a pencil, to show it will be the first aicme - first few disk.

Next look at the few for the letter 'L' and do the same thing. Work your way through the entire set until you have disks for each few. By having extra disks, you will have a better chance of picking the right one and not having to settle for the "last ones" when you get near the end. I recommend getting two bags and using all of the disks from both bags in this selection process and then use the ones that were *NOT* selected to practice on.

Practice is the next step in the process. Using the left over disks, try making the letters and symbols you put on the discs. Since these practice disks are going to be discarded after the practice, feel free to fill them up as much as possible. When you are confident in your ability, it is time to move on to the next phase, which is laying out the disks.

You can trace the format from a copy of the following pages, directly on the disk by placing carbon paper between the paper and disk. Make sure to hold the disk down firmly while doing the tracing. Any mistakes can be washed off after the lettering is done.

With your disks now completed, the next step is to find the proper container for them. Some people like to keep their disks in a nicely decorated bag, others in a leather pouch, and others tied up in a cloth. Until you have the permanent "home" for the disks, you can store them in a zip-lock bag so they do not get lost.

Some people feel that a 'cleansing' step should be added in at this point. My personal opinion is that it is not necessary and that your working with the tool is the only 'cleansing' that is needed. If you do want to fully cleanse the disks after they have been made, I would recommend leaving them exposed for a few hours to the light of the full moon, and then to the full noonday sun.

The last step in the process is to attune your subconscious 'fully' with the disks. Wait until after you have them in their permanent pouch. There is really no hurry in doing it until you are ready to work with them. For the attuning, place them under your mattress for at least a week. This will give your "dreaming mind" a chance to fully connect with the tools and make your readings appear to you easier. After the week, they are ready to use and you should be able to get a good reading as soon as you start using them!

Hand made sets, made by myself using this method, are available for sale on my website at: http://tinyurl.com/2epegy.

(This appendix is from The Way of the Trees Magical Training System, © 2001 by Rev. Skip Ellison.)

Appendix 2 - Making Your Own Ogham Discs

The First Aicme

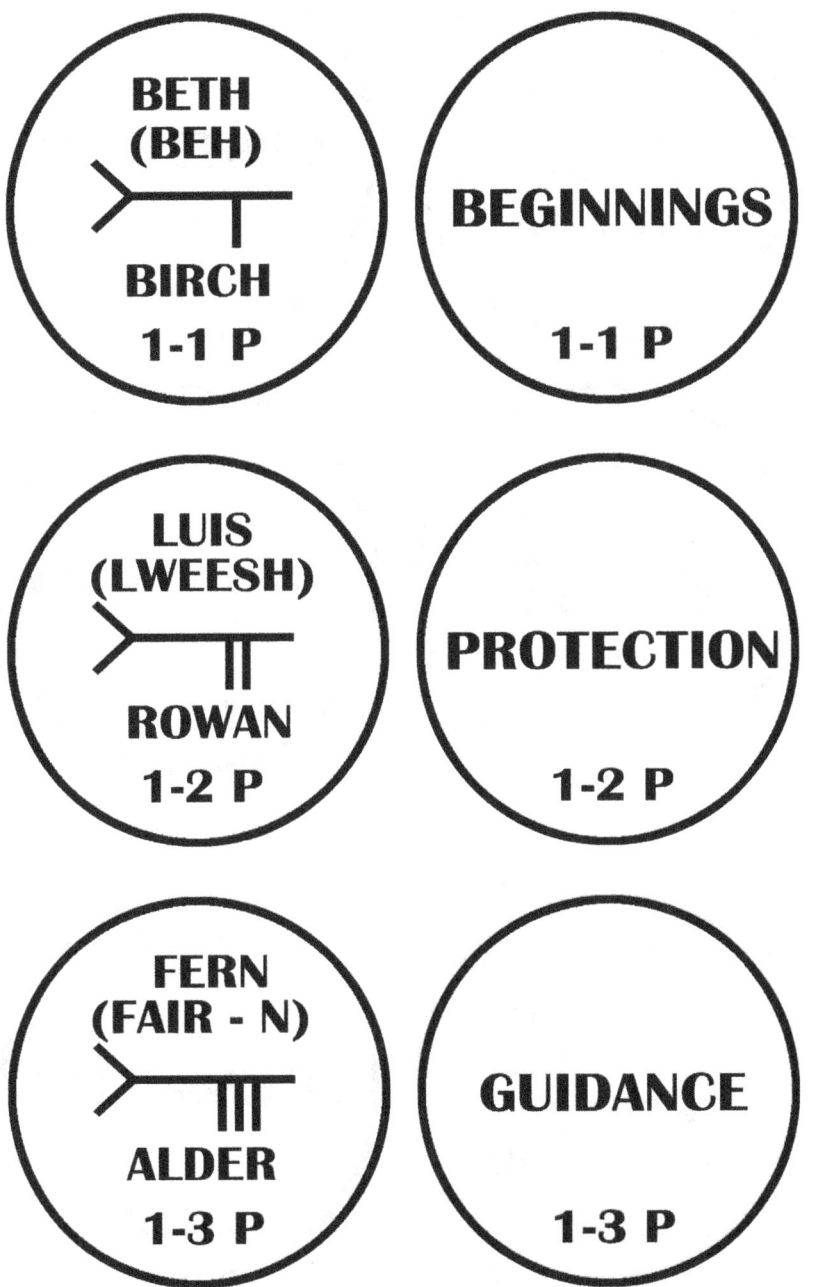

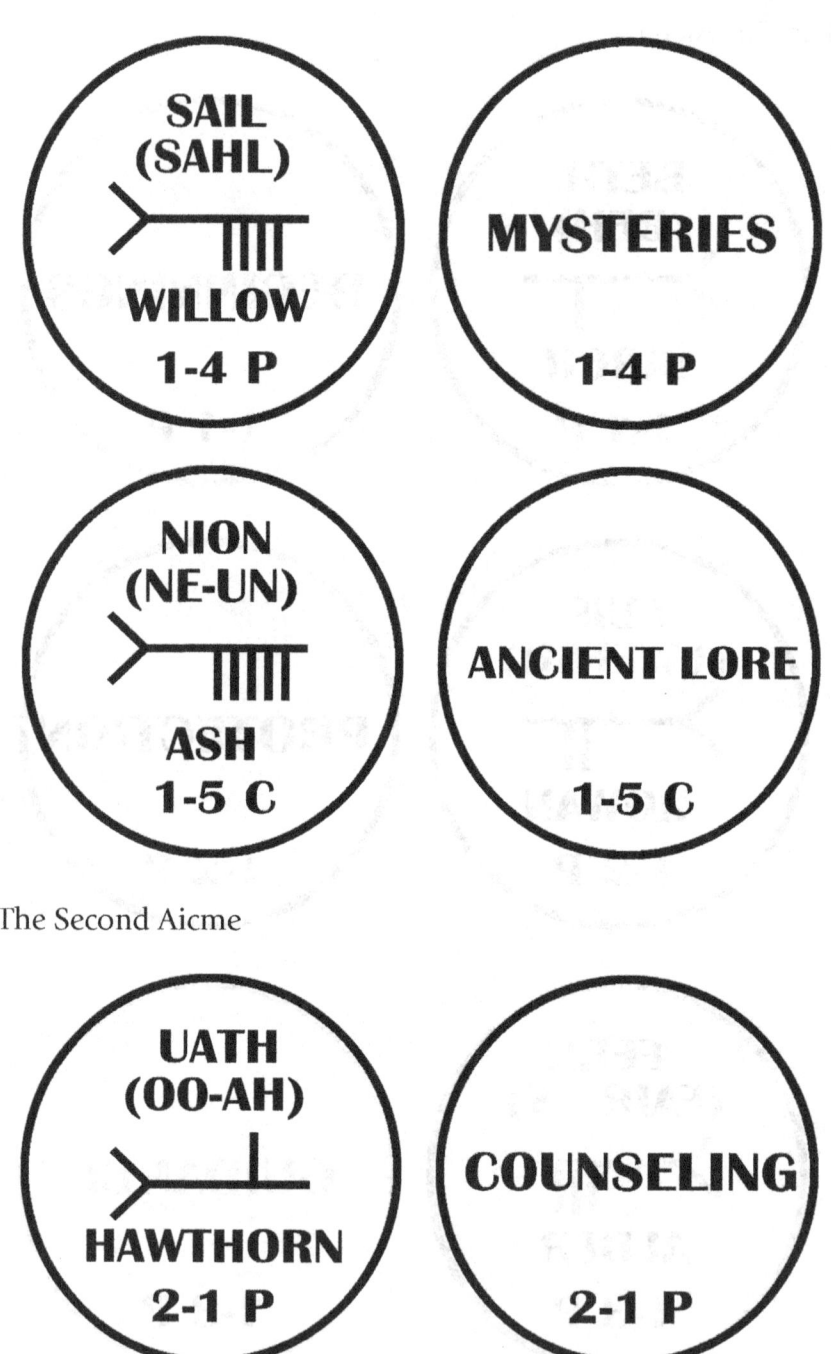

The Second Aicme

Appendix 2 - Making Your Own Ogham Discs

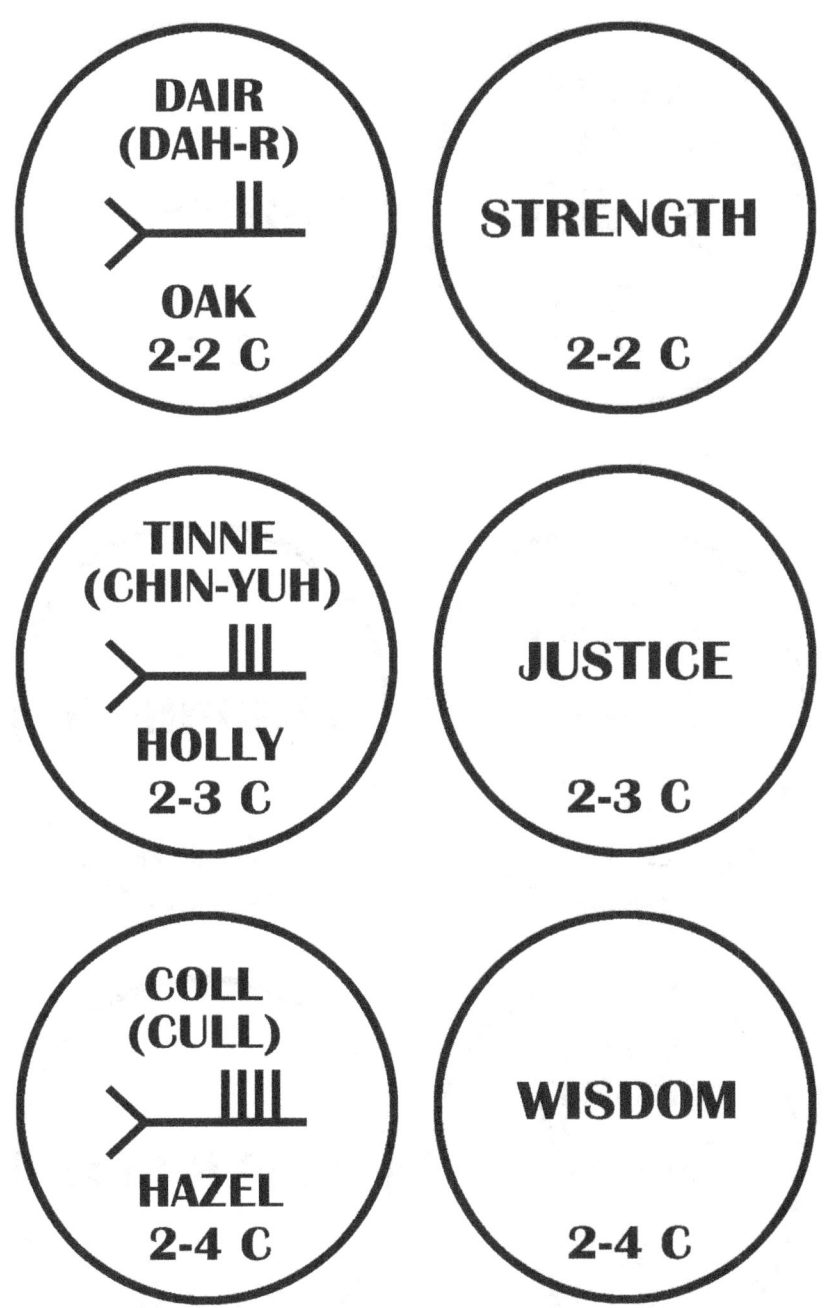

The Third Aicme

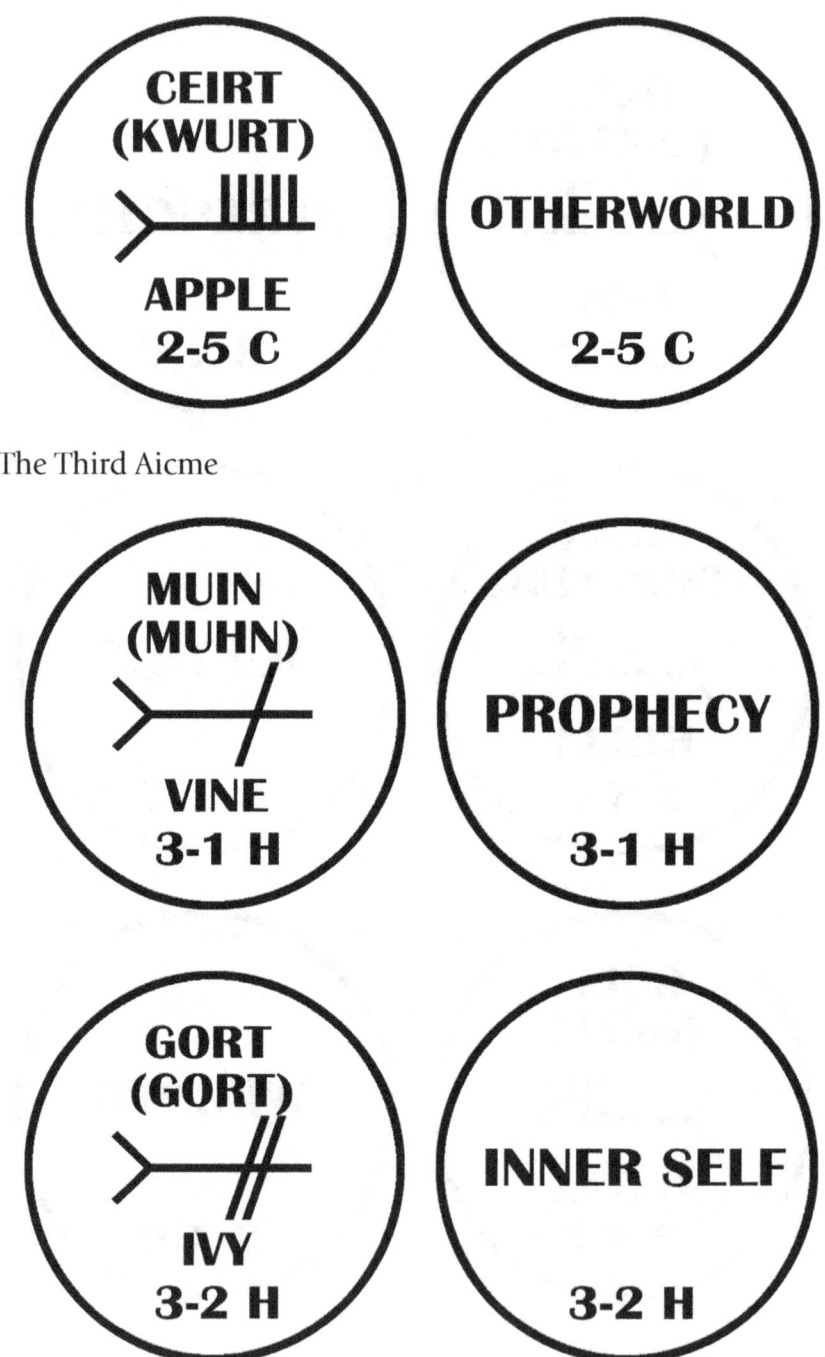

Appendix 2 - Making Your Own Ogham Discs

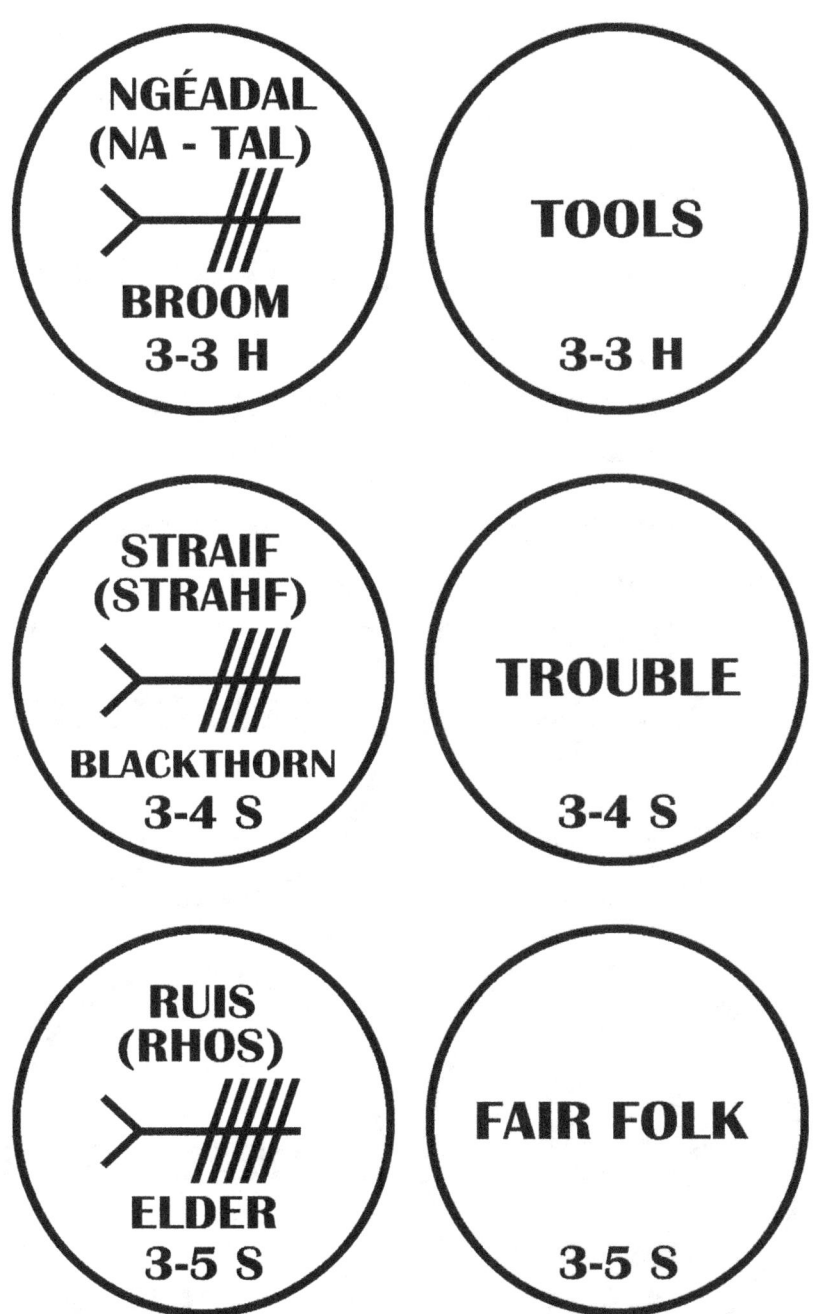

135

The Fourth Aicme

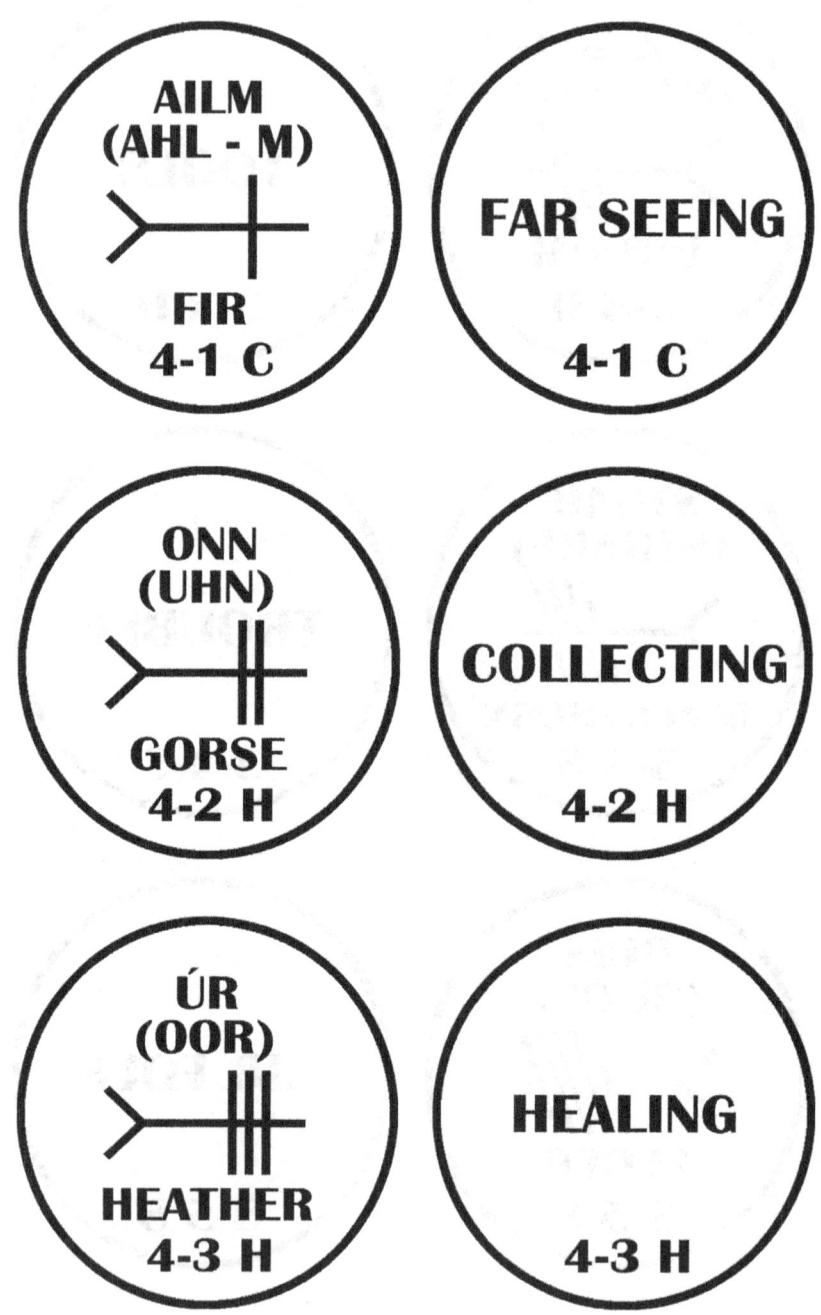

Appendix 2 - Making Your Own Ogham Discs

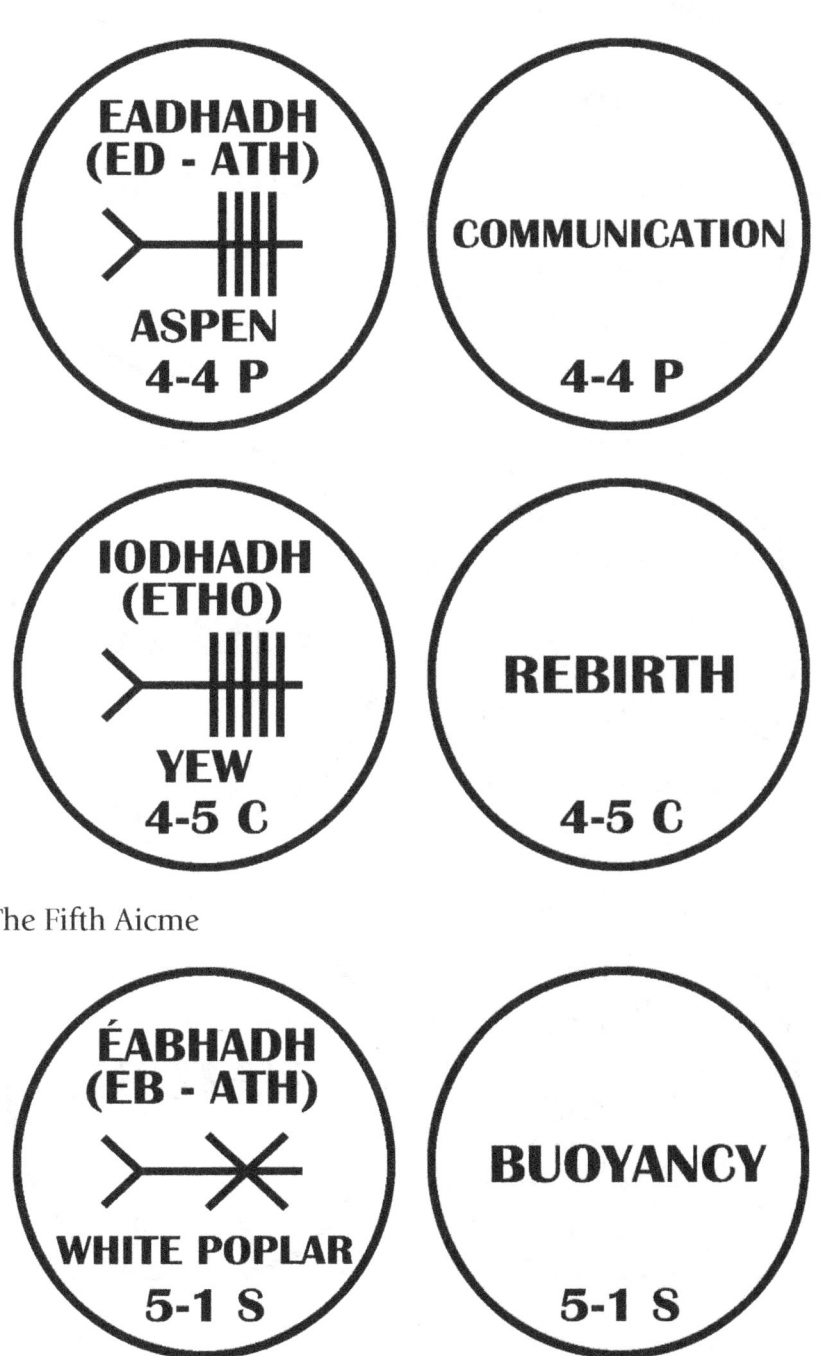

The Fifth Aicme

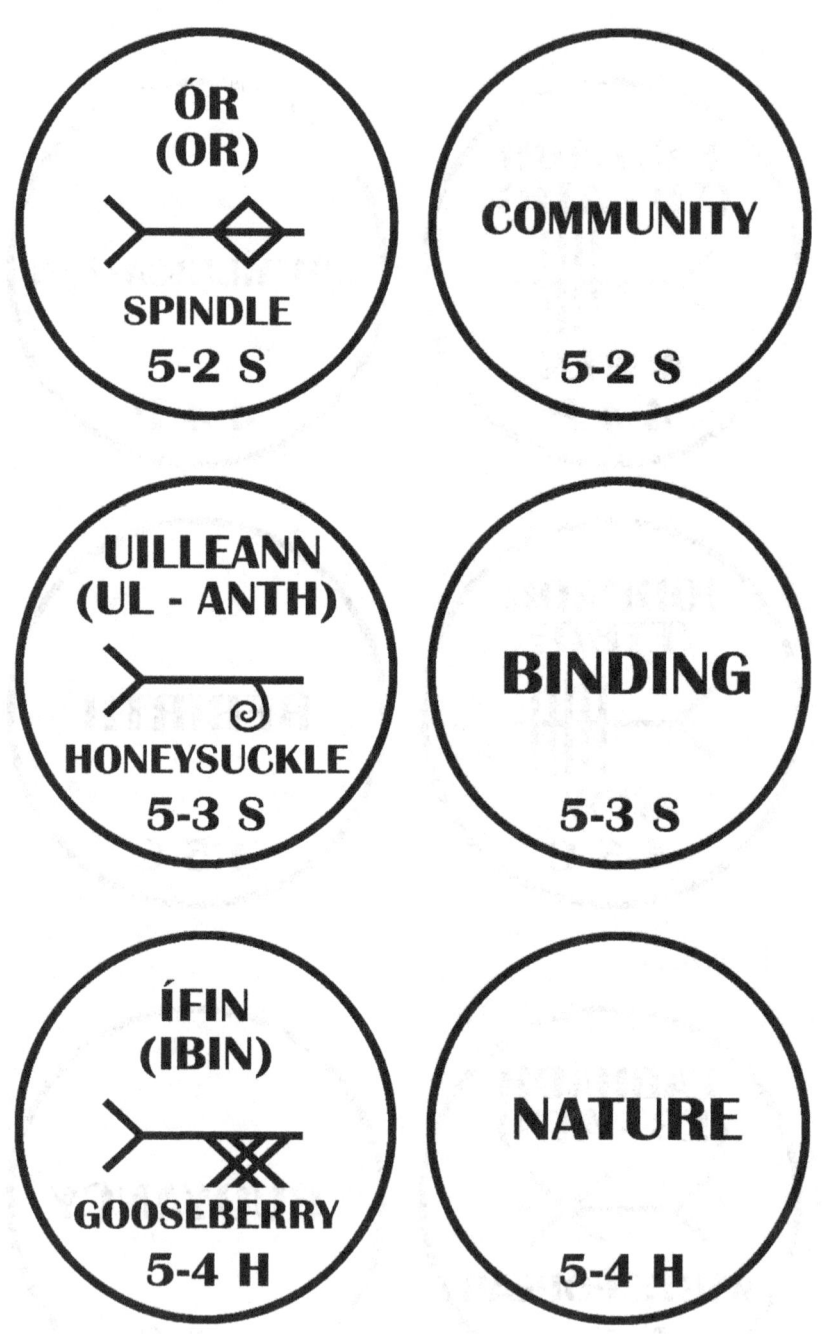

Appendix 2 - Making Your Own Ogham Discs

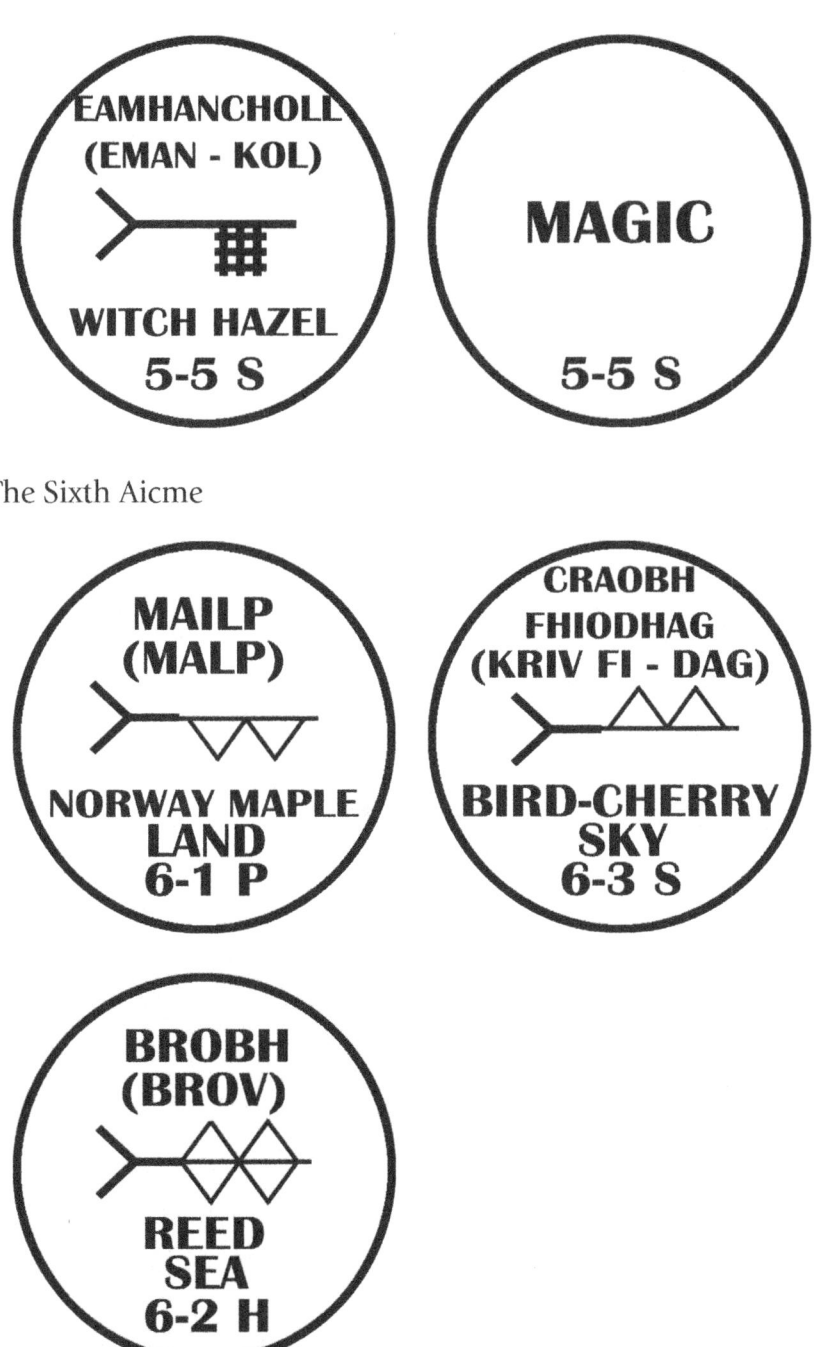

The Sixth Aicme

Appendix 3

Resources

Print

Much of my information on the oghams comes from *Auraicept Na N-éces: A Scholars' Primer* edited by George Calder in 1917. It is sub-titled "Being the texts of the ogham tract from the Book of Ballymote and the Yellow Book of Lecan, and the text of the Trefhocul from the Book of Leinster." My edition is from the 1995 reprint by Four Courts Press, US branch located in Portland Oregon, ISBN - 1851821813. While this book is expensive, currently $75, it is VERY valuable and can be ordered at the following site: http://www.fourcourts-press.ie/cgi/bookshow.cgi?file=a_eces.xml. The Scholar's Primer has the advantage of having the Irish on one page with the English translation on the facing page. And it is considered by most scholars as being one of the best texts available on the oghams.

Another important "masterwork" on oghams is *Corpus Inscriptionum Insularum Celticarum* by Robert Alexander Stewart (R.A.S.) Macalister. It was reprinted by Four Courts Press, UK branch located in Dublin, Ireland in 1996, with ISBN - 1851822429. This book is available through the following link, http://www.amazon.com/exec/obidos/ASIN/1851822429/dragonskeepfa-20. This book lists and shows, usually in line drawings, all of the ogham inscriptions found in the British Isles at the time it was first published in 1945. It's an expensive book, also currently $75, but I feel it is well worth it.

Macalister's work was followed up in *A Guide to Ogham* written by Damien McManus. It was published by Leinster Leader Ltd., of Kildare, Ireland in 1991. ISBN – 1870684753. This book was written to correct errors and update the findings of RAS Macalister. As such, it really needs to be used with "Corpus Inscriptionum Insularum Celticarum". In fact, this, the Macalister book and the Swift book, talked about next, should all be used together. his book is available through the following link, http://www.amazon.com/exec/obidos/ASIN/1870684753/dragonskeepfa-20.

One of McManus's students, Catherine Swift, followed up his book with one of her own titled, *Ogham Stones and the Earliest Irish Christians*. This was published by The Cardinal Press, Maynooth OK in 1997 with ISBN – 0901519987. This book is available through the following link, http://www.amazon.com/exec/obidos/ASIN/0901519987/dragonskeepfa-20. This book was written to correct some errors and amplify on the work of Damien McManus. It's a very worthwhile book to own and gives many insights into what the Ogham was originally used for. It also includes the translations from Old Irish for many of the names used on the Ogham stones, something I feel that is important enough to justify its cost.

While looking at the tree ogham and its several variants in the 'other oghams', it is important to gain an understanding of the trees they were working with when it was in use. A good book to help with this is *Collins Wild Guide – Trees of Britain and Ireland* edited by Bob Press. It was published by Harper Collins Publishers, of Milan Italy in 1996. The ISBN is 0002200090. This book is available through the following link, http://www.amazon.com/exec/obidos/ASIN/0002200090/dragonskeepfa-20. This book talks about the actual trees that are in Britain and Ireland now and used in conjunction with the next book in the list, you can find the trees that lived there during the 4th century CE.

Another very good book dealing with the spread of the trees through Europe is *Proto-Indo-European Trees* by Paul Friedrich, published by the University of Chicago Press in 1970. The ISBN is 0226264807. It is available through the following link, http://www.amazon.com/exec/obidos/ASIN/0226264807/dragonskeepfa-20. This is a Master's thesis that traces the spread of trees throughout Europe by means of pollen data. It is an excellent work for knowing when individual types of trees appeared in the different areas. Not all of the trees in the ogham are covered but it's a good start.

Several "popularized" books on ogham are worth buying. One is *The New Celtic Oracle* by Nigel Pennick and Nigel Jackson. It was published by Aquarian Press, London in 1997, with an ISBN of 1898307563. This book is available through the following link, http://www.amazon.com/exec/obidos/ASIN/1898307563/dragonskeepfa-20. This is a fairly good book with lots of information on the oghams.

While I am talking about "popularized" books, there is one that many people ask questions about. That is *The White Goddess* by Robert Graves. This book has a large section on the ogham, but all of his work needs to be read with a critical eye. His specialty was Greek poetry, not Irish or Welsh history and he admits that in his book. Graves was the person who 'invented' the association of the trees with times of the year – The Tree Calendar. Not very many scholars take this work seriously. A reprint edition came out in January of 1966 by Farrar, Straus and Giroux, ISBN – 0374504938. This book is available through the following link, http://www.amazon.com/exec/obidos/ASIN/0374504938/dragonskeepfa-20.

Appendix 3 - Resources

Web

Now we move on to web sources. As with any popular subject, there are many, many sites dealing with the oghams. A Google search for the word 'oghams' shows 20,600 hits! Obviously, not all of them are good sites. There are some sites that are worthwhile, and I'll include a few here.

Clark, Curtis – http://www.intranet.csupomona.edu/~jcclark/ogham/oghtree.html. 1998. A natural history of the trees of the Ogham compiled in 1995. While I do not agree with all of his interpretations, the site is worthwhile.

Everson, Michael - http://www.evertype.com/standards/og/ogmharc.html - Everything Ogham on the Web. This is just what the name says, it has it all!

Everson, Michael - Standards - http://www.evertype.com/standards/og/n037.html - The naming standards for the Oghams.

http://www.ucl.ac.uk/archaeology/cisp/database/ - This is the database that includes all of the information about the Celtic inscribed stones, their location, when and where they have been referred to in literature and their possible translations. A VERY good database to work with!

Liberty – The Ogham Stone – http://ogham.lyberty.com/ - A very nice site with many wonderful pictures.

Ravenbard - http://www.geocities.com/Area51/Nebula/1241/vogham1.html - An interesting "virtual tour" of the Ogham.

CELT literature project - http://www.ucc.ie/celt/published/T302018/index.html - " *Buile Suibhne* (The Frenzy of Suibhne) being The Adventures of *Suibhne Geilt."* This Irish tale is a VERY good source of *hidden* material about the oghams. In it, Suibhne, son of Colman Cuar, king of *Dal Araidhe* becomes crazed during a battle and goes to live in the forest. As he sleeps or hides in different trees, he talks about the tree. The language is not very plain in this, remember it was part of the 'hidden lore,' but interesting bits can be teased out to give you an insight into the tree. More of the hidden lore can be found in my book in the section on the "Battle of the Trees."

Today, most of my research on the oghams comes from academic journals or from the original manuscripts. My favorite tool to find the articles is Google Scholar, http://scholar.google.com/. Typing in the word ogham here lists 313 articles on the subject, but the real value comes from word combinations, such as ogham divination (43 articles) or ogham boundary marker (25 articles). One downside of using this resource is that many of the articles found are on the JSTOR site. The description of JSTOR from its website reads:

> "JSTOR is a not-for-profit organization with a dual mission to create and maintain a trusted archive of important scholarly journals, and to provide access to these journals as widely as possible. JSTOR offers researchers the ability to retrieve high-resolution, scanned images of journal issues and pages as they were originally designed, printed, and illustrated."[1]

This site needs to be accessed through a local university or college, but many colleges will allow access to non-students for a small fee or may even offer free access in the library itself.

For accessing the original manuscripts, when I wrote my ogham book in 2003, there were no digital scans available online. I had to write the Royal Irish Academy in Dublin and buy copies of high quality photographs of each page and scan them in myself. Today, you can go to Irish Scripts On Screen, http://www.isos.dias.ie/english/index.html, and after joining the organization and getting a login, download high quality scans that print out well enough to be read with no trouble. All of the original material dealing with the oghams, which I know about at least, is now available there.

---

[1] From http://www.jstor.org/about/desc.html

Appendix 4
Working with the Old Irish

Almost all of the ancient ogham inscriptions, other than the Pictish inscriptions, have to be translated into Old Irish from the ogham. Then the Old Irish has to be translated into English, or some other modern language. Learning Old Irish is, at least to me, a difficult process. There are a few books dealing with the subject and some schools offer courses in it, usually associated with a Celtic Studies program.

One book that I've found helpful for the grammar is *An Introduction to Old Irish* by R.P.M and W.P. Lehmann. This was published by the Modern Language Association of America, located in New York City in 1975, and reprinted in 1999. Its ISBN is 0873522885 and it can be ordered through the following link, http://www.amazon.com/exec/obidos/ASIN/0873522885/dragonskeepfa-20. While this book does have a glossary, it usually isn't too helpful with the words found on the inscriptions.

The absolute best source I have found for vocabulary is the *Dictionary of the Irish Language,* edited by E. G. Quin. This is a very expensive book, usually in the $90 + range and can be ordered using the following link, http://www.amazon.com/exec/obidos/ASIN/0901714291/dragonskeepfa-20, if there are any available. Many times, it can be located in university libraries and consulted there. Unfortunately, I do not own this book so I couldn't scan in the cover. It is on my wish list though!

Fortunately, there are a few free online resources. I have them listed here.

- http://digitalmedievalist.com/faqs/oldirish.html#method – This site is the best list of how to go about learning Old Irish that I have found. It is kept current and has many resources listed!
- http://www.utexas.edu/cola/centers/lrc/eieol/iriol-0-X.html - This site, opened in 2007, was created at the University of Texas, Austin by the team of Patrizia de Bernardo Stempel, Caren Esser, and Jonathan Slocum. While I have not worked through all the lessons yet, it does look very good!
- http://www.ceantar.org/Dicts/MB2/index.html - MacBain's Etymological Dictionary of the Gaelic Language is very helpful for finding the meaning of Old Irish words. Al-

though the primary language is Modern Irish, it lists many of the Old Irish words the modern words were derived from. I usually use the 'search on this page' function of my browser to find the word I'm looking for.
- http://www.ceantar.org/Dicts/ - This is a listing of the modern Scots, Irish and Manx language dictionaries online. Sometimes, by searching those dictionaries, you can find the Old Irish word, or something very similar, that you are looking for.

Knowledge of Modern Irish is helpful and that is easier to obtain. In many locations, native speaking teachers can be found, plus there are several websites devoted to teaching beginners. One good one is:

- http://www.daltai.com - This is the Irish language information and resources site. It has sections for vocabulary and proverbs along with forums where you can get help and find teachers.

Once you have the basics of the language, the next step is learning how to pronounce the words. Again, this is a difficult process, at least for me. One of the best guides to pronunciation I have found is in *Dictionary of Celtic Mythology* by James MacKillop, which was published by the Oxford University Press in 1998. Its ISBN is 0198691572 and it can be ordered through this link, http://www.amazon.com/exec/obidos/ASIN/0198691572/dragonskeepfa-20. This book is referenced on many of the academic lists and is highly thought of.

As with all pronunciation guides, this method of learning to *speak* the language is nowhere near as good as working with someone who has learned to speak the language in a classroom setting, where they can get feedback from the instructor, but at least it is close.

Another good guide can be found online at http://www.smo.uhi.ac.uk/old-irish/labhairt.html. This guide was created by Dennis King, a very helpful person in the Old Irish community! Dennis is also the list owner and moderator for the Old Irish L e-list. More information about the list, which is very open to helping beginners, can be found at http://w3.lincolnu.edu/~focal/docs/old-irish-list.htm. Catherine Swift, who wrote *Ogham Stones and the Earliest Irish Christians*, is also usually active on this list.

Appendix 4 - Working with the Old Irish

1. Examples from the surviving stones.

As Macalister tells us in the introduction to his book, there are nine basic Old Irish formats used in stone inscriptions[1]. They are:

A. Single names where it usually is thought to be the person who erected the stone.

B. Single names with AMA preceding the name. This is thought to indicate that the stone is the grave marker for the person named.

C. The name of the person commemorated and their father. This is expressed as (name) MAQI (name). The MAQI is the early form of the Old Irish *mac*, which means 'son'. It is sometimes seen in inscriptions as MAQQI, MACI, MAC or MAQ.

D. The name of the person commemorated and their grandfather. This is expressed as (name) AVI (name). The AVI is the early form of the Old Irish *aui*, meaning grandson or descendant.

E. The name of the person commemorated and their uncle. This is expressed as (name) NETA (name). The NETA is the early form of the Old Irish *nia*, meaning nephew. It is sometimes seen in inscriptions as NETTA or NIOTTA.

F. The name of the person commemorated and their patron. This is expressed as (name) CELI (name). The CELI is the early form of the Old Irish *céle*, meaning follower or client or devotee.

G. The name of the person commemorated and one of their remote ancestors. This is expressed as (name) MAQI MUCOI (name). This may also be seen as (name) MUCOI (name). The MUCOI is the early form of the Old Irish *maccu* or *moccu*, which means descendant.

H. The name of the person commemorated and their father and a remote ancestor. This is expressed as (name) MAQI (name) MAQI MUCOI (name).

I. The use of the word KOI with (name) MAQI MUCOI (name) to give us (name) KOI MAQI MUCOI (name). It is possible that this means 'the' main descendant of, instead of 'one of' the descendants.

---

1 Macalister, R.A.S. *Corpus Inscriptionum Insularum Celticarum.* Four Courts Press, Dublin, Ireland. 1996 edition. ISBN 1-85182-242-9 Page 56 & 57

With these forms in mind, let's work through the translations of a few actual inscriptions. As a reminder, here is the diagram showing what the oghams translate to.

ᚅ	N	ᚆ	Q	ᚉ	R	ᚊ	I	ᚋ	AE, X, XI
ᚄ	S	ᚈ	C	ᚌ	Z	ᚍ	E	ᚎ	PH, IO
ᚃ	F	ᚇ	T	ᚏ	Y	ᚐ	U	ᚑ	UI, P, PE
ᚂ	L	ᚑ	D	ᚒ	G	ᚓ	O	ᚔ	OI, TH
ᚁ	B	ᚕ	H	ᚖ	M	ᚗ	A	ᚘ	EA, CH, KH

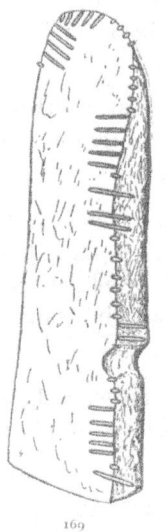

169

For this first inscription, we will use an example from *Corpus Inscriptionum Insularum Celticarum* (CIIC). This example is numbered 169 and is found on page 163. It is located in Killarney in County Kerry at the St. Brendan's Seminary.

This is translated by Macalister as, starting on the bottom and reading up, MAQI (with part of the 'I' missing), followed by LIAG MAQI ERCA. From this we can assume that a lower part of the stone is missing, which matches what Macalister learned from the local people. This lower part would have had another name on it to show 'the person's name that' was the son of Liag, a personal name, who was the son of Erca, another personal name. MacManus translates the Liag as from the Old Irish *liac*, meaning stone and the Erca as from the Old Irish *Erciyas*, with no meaning given.[2]

This next example is also from Macalister, is numbered 215 and is found on page 209. This example is also located in County Kerry.

This is translated by Macalister as reading ALATTO CELI BATTIGNI. He assumes, rightly I believe, that the writer was confused by the curve of the

---

2 From http://www.ucl.ac.uk/archaeology/cisp/database/stone/bragh_2.html - 1/17/06.

Appendix 4 - Working with the Old Irish

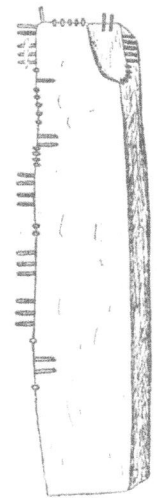

stone and placed a Q, going to the left of the line as you are reading down, instead of the N, which should come off to the right of the line reading down, that would make more sense in the personal name. This is a tricky transition and a mistake that is commonly made. In English, this would translate as Alatto, a personal name, who is the follower of Battigni, another personal name. McManus believes that the name Allato may come from the Old Irish *allaid*, meaning wild and the name Battigni may come from the Old Irish *báethíne* or *báeth*, meaning foolish.[3]

Our last translation is also from Macalister. It is numbered 254 and is found on page 248. It is now located in the National Museum of Ireland and was originally from County Kerry.

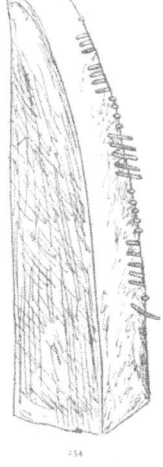

Macalister translates this as MAQI RECTA, which would be son of Recta. The description of the stone does list it as having part split off, which would likely contain the rest of the inscription. The name Recta has not been translated but does have a masculine ending.

Using these examples, we have seen the basic process for translating actual inscriptions. Using this same technique in reverse, you can easily create your own inscriptions using Old Irish, if you want to be authentic, or in English if, you want to make it easier for people to understand.

---

3 From http://www.ucl.ac.uk/archaeology/cisp/database/stone/whfl d_1.html - 1/17/06

Appendix 5
A Word about Ár nDraíocht Féin

Ár nDraíocht Féin is Modern Irish for 'Our Own Druidism' and is a play on words for 'our own magic.' Most people just call it 'ADF.' Isaac Bonewits and a group of other Neopagans interested in researching and reviving the ways of worship of the early Indo-European peoples founded ADF.

Isaac had been associated with several other religious organizations and wanted to develop an organization that better fit his vision for the future. His vision was that one day Neopagan Druidism would be as readily accepted as any other mainstream religion. He believed (and still does) that there should be a local grove in every city.

Isaac is the author of *Real Magic* (a classic work on the laws of magic), *Authentic Thaumaturgy* (an adaptation of the laws of magic for role-playing games), *Rites of Worship* (an instruction manual for creating and performing public worship rites), plus several other new or forthcoming books. He is also a very talented Bard and an inveterate, unrepentant punster!

ADF, founded in 1984, incorporated as a non-profit religious organization on April 18, 1987. Registered in the state of Delaware as a Nonprofit Corporation, it has 501(c)3, tax-exempt status, from the IRS in the USA. This tax-exempt status has been extended to many of our local groves through a group exemption and these groves have qualified as private foundations, as outlined in articles 509(a)1 and 170(b)1(A)(l) of the Federal tax code.

I lead ADF today, as its third Archdruid, a position I've held since May of 2001. I belong to and lead a 'Mother Grove' that acts as its board of directors.

Locally, there are solitairies, protogroves, provisionally chartered groves, and fully chartered groves. Three officers, usually called the Senior Druid, Secretary, and Treasurer, lead a grove. There can also be several other officers, such as a Bard, Preceptor, Chronicler, Liturgist, Herbalist, Healer, Ecologist, etc., but they are not required.

"Solitairies" are ADF members who live in areas where there are no other ADF members, where no one is interested is starting a proto-grove, or simply are individuals who choose not to participate in the local groves in their area. Much of the activity in ADF is happening online, so solitairies with computer access do have a large support network online, even if they do not participate in any grove's activities.

ADF currently has about 60 active Groves and protogroves that are meeting, worshipping, and attracting new members. Our membership is a little over 1100 and growing steadily in the US, Canada and several other countries. The membership has been growing slowly but steadily, since ADF's incorporation on April 18, 1987.

As an organization, we honor all the Indo-European pantheons (Celtic, Norse, Hellenic, Roman, Slavic, Baltic, etc.). Individual Groves and members can choose to honor just one pantheon or several if they desire, as long as they are Indo-European.

Many of the ADF Neopagan Druids today subscribe to most of the following beliefs:

- We believe that divinity is both within and all around us, immanent and transcendent.
- We believe that it is most important to pay attention to the divinity within ourselves at this critical juncture for the Earth.
- We believe in a multiplicity of Gods and Goddesses, equal in power and status, as well as in a host of lesser beings, known by many names (Nature Spirits, Fairy Folk, Ancestors, etc.).
- We believe it is necessary to honor and respect the Earth Mother as the living being she is. We also hold ecological awareness and activism to be sacred duties.
- We believe that ethics and morality should be based on love, joy, self-esteem, mutual respect, the avoidance of actual harm to others and ourselves, and to the increase of public benefit.
- We believe that humans were meant to lead lives filled with joy, love, pleasure, beauty and humor.
- We believe that with proper training, we are able to perform most of the magic and miracles we are ever likely to need.
- We believe in the importance of celebrating the solar, lunar and other cycles in our lives.
- Most of us believe in reincarnation with a time of resting and learning in-between incarnations.

- We believe that to live in society, you must give back to society through community service.

One feature that many people are interested in is our Study Program. One of ADF's mottoes is 'Why not Excellence?' We believe that the best way to promote excellence is by having a program that teaches people about the many facets of ADF and of how we practice Our Own Druidry. For the last five or six years, we have been changing our Study Program to make it more user-friendly and better suited for the organization and its members. We made a great deal of progress on it, but another of our mottoes is, 'As fast as a speeding oak!' It seems that we're living up to that one!

The first step in our Study Program, the Dedicant Path, is about a yearlong course of study in Our Druidism. As well as defining for themselves the nine virtues, students learn meditation techniques, study Indo-European cultures, learn about and perform rituals, learn about the High Days, construct and start using a home shrine, and start working with the local land spirits. The student also starts using a journal to document work done and rituals attended. People have been working through this program since the summer of 1999, and ADF now has many members who have completed the Dedicant's Program. For many people, the Dedicant Path is a road to travel, not a journey to complete. If a student does not want to go further in our Study Programs, the working on the Dedicant Path is fulfilling in itself. After completing the Dedicant's Program, people have four choices. They can enroll in one or more of the following:

- The Initiate's Program is a program designed for those who wish to either expand their training beyond the ADF Dedicant Path, but do not want a purely academic course of study, or are unsure if they are interested in becoming ADF Clergy. All the courses in this program will count toward the Clergy Training Program (CTP).
- The Clergy Council of ADF designed, and administers the CTP. This program has three ranks, identified as "circles," with the goal of producing fully trained, ordainable ADF clergy. After the completion of the First Circle, with the addition of one other course, the student attains the status of Dedicant Priest. At the completion of the Third Circle, the student is ordained as a Full Priest of ADF.
- The Generalist Study Program (GSP) provides an understanding of the history of druidism and ADF, comparative mythology, and a chosen cultural focus. The GSP is weighted academically, and students should balance this with spiritual and religious work, such as continued medi-

tation and High Day observation from the DP. This program is designed and administered by the ADF Preceptor with the assistance of the recognized Guilds.
- Lastly, the training programs designed by official Guilds of ADF, under the supervision of the ADF Preceptor and the Council of Lore, with rank advancements being identified as circles.

The Initiate's program is open and has been accepting students, since the fall of 2006.

The Clergy Training Program is open and has been accepting students, since May of 2005.

The ADF Generalist Study Program is open, and has been accepting students, since July of 2003.

The Guilds are the backbone of the main section of ADF's Study Program. They are the repository of our lore and are the resource that provides the training. The Guilds (specialties) currently in place for the ADF Study Program are:

> First Function — Bardic, Liturgist, Magician, Seer and Scholar.
> Second Function — Warrior.
> Third Function — Artisan, Brewers, Dance, Healer, and Naturalist.

ADF can be reached on the web at www.adf.org or by snail mail at P.O. Box 17874, Tucson, AZ 85731-7874.

Index

Æ 43, 93
Abbreviations #1 Ogham 63
Abbreviations #2 Ogham 63
Abies alba 43
Acaint. .... See Aconite
Acer negundo 41
Acer platanoides 59
Aconite 44
Adamnan 24, 94
Adder 22
Adze 27
Aed 44, 94
African Alphabet Ogham 75
Agricola 6
Agricultural Ogham 13, 93
Aidhircleóg .... See Lapwing
Ailim .... See Ailm
Ailm 43, 126
Aimitis .... See Amethyst
Airchetul .... See Poetry
Airgead....................... See Silver
Airigeacht .... See Sovereignty
Alad .... See Piebald
Alder 17, 122, 125
Aliter Ogham 80
Alnus glutinosa 17
Amethyst 44
Anguish of a Poet's Heart Ogham 67
Anvil 51
Apple 31, 32, 121
Aquamarine 35
Arathar .... See Plough
Arcán .... See Piglet
Arms Ogham 99
Art Ogham 13, 94
Aru 43, 92
Ár nDraíocht Féin 155
Asal .... See Donkey
Ash 15, 21, 22, 122, 125

Aspen 49, 50, 53, 126
Athair .... See Yarrow
Atucmlu 7
Auraicept na n-Éces 1
Axe 13
Bairgen .... See Bread
Bán .... See White
Barrow 5, 13, 92
Basket 41
Battle of the Trees .. 17, 113, 114, 118, 121, 144
Bearna 60
Beiril .... See Beryl
Beith 11, 13, 125
Beithe 9, 10
Beltaine 56
Bend (or Angle) Ogham 71
Beryl 14
Besan .... See Pheasant
Beth 125
Bethumnacht ...... See Livelihood
Betula pendula 13
Biail .... See Axe
Billhook 49
Birch 13, 14, 125
Bird Cherry 60, 126
Bird Ogham 5, 13, 93
Black 25, 119
Blackthorn 39, 40, 125
Blind Man Ogham 76
Bloodstone 31
Blue 35
Bóv .... See Cow
Boar 27
Boat Ogham 100
Bodhran 108
Bonewits, Isaac 155
Book of Ballymote, The . 1, 61, 141
Book of Leinster, The 1, 4, 141
Box Elder 41

155

Boy Ogham 6, 62, 96
Braisech .... *See* Kale
Bran 17, 18, 81, 94, 125
Brass work 47
Brehon Laws 13
Brenainn 13, 94
Briatharogam Con Culainn 10
Bright 39
Brobh 59, 126
Bronze 17
Broom 37, 38, 125
Brown 29
Bruden 13, 92
Buile Suibhne 10, 143
Byrony 47
Câd Goddeu 113, 114, 118, 121
Calluna vulgaris 47
Canal Ogham 79
Carr .... *See* Wagon
Cask 25
Cat's Eye 19
Catt 29, 92
Ceirt 31, 125
Cera 29, 92
Cert .... *See* Ceirt
Cherry 60, 126
Chestnut 35, 123
Chieftain trees 13, 21, 25, 27, 29, 31, 43, 51
Church Ogham 93
Ciaran 31, 94
Cinquefoil 31
Clear 21
Cloch Fhola .... *See* Bloodstone
Clooties 20
Colaimbin .... *See* Columbine
Coll 29, 87, 125
Coll Ogham 87
Color Ogham 13, 93
Columbine 29
Combative Ogham 86
Company Ogham 101
Conjunct Ogham 82
Connacht 4, 110

Copar .... *See* Copper
Copper 29, 47
Corann 31, 92
Corn-field Ogham 87
Corpus Inscriptionum Insularum Celti carum 7, 103, 141, 147, 148
Corr Mhóna .... *See* Crane
Corylus avellana 29
Cow 13, 98
Cow Ogham 98
Crab Apple 31
Crane 29
Crannchur 7
Craobh Fhiodhag 60, 126
Crataegus monogyna 23
Cricket 31
Criogar .... *See* Cricket
Cron .... *See* Brown
Cronan 29, 94
Cruitireacht .... *See* Harping
Cú .... *See* Hound
Cual .... *See* Faggot
Cualand 43, 93
Cúchulainn 4, 5, 10, 13, 15, 17, 19, 21, 23, 25, 27, 29, 31, 33, 35, 37, 39, 41, 43, 45, 47, 49, 51, 53, 55
Cúige 109
Cuiqbhileach .... *See* Cinquefoil
Cusrat 31, 92
Cytisus scoparius 37
Dabach .... *See* Cask
Dagda 103
Dair 25, 125
Daisy 37
Dallán 103
Damh .... *See* Ox
Dark Grey 27
Deer-stalking 39
Dergderg 25, 92
Diamant .... *See* Diamond
Diamond 25
Dinn Ríg 25, 92

Diphthong Group Behind Us
  Ogham 78
Dispensing 41
Dog Ogham 98
Donkey 44
Donnan 25, 94
Droen .... *See* Wren
Drualus .... *See* Mistletoe
Druidheacht .... *See* Wizardry
Dub .... *See* Black
Duck 5, 93
Duir .... *See* Dair
Dun 45
Éabhadh 53, 126
Eadha .... *See* Eadhadh
Eadhadh 49, 126
Eaglet 51
Eamhancholl 58
Early Irish Letter-Names 9
Eascann .... *See* Eel
Ebad ..... 67, 88. *See also* Éabhadh
Ébad. .... *See* Éabhadh
Ebad-fashioned Ogham ... 67, 88
Edad .... *See* Eadhadh
Eel 49
Egyptian (Hebrew) Ogham ... 74
Eibhear .... *See* Granite
Eileabar .... *See* Hellebore
Eite 60, 126
Ela .... *See* Swan
Elder 41, 42, 126
Elderberry 41, 42
Emancholl ...... *See* Eamhancholl
Enaireacht .... *See* Fowling
Enclosed Ogham 68
End to End Ogham 86
English Ivy 35
English Oak 25
Eobul 45, 92
Eochaid Ollathair ..... *See* Dagda
Epit .... *See* Billhook
Erbus 49, 92
Erc .... *See* Red
Ernen 49, 94

Étáine 103
Euonymus europaeus 55
European Alder 17
European Honeysuckle 56
European Mountain Ash 15
Eyebright 41
Fælinn .... *See* Gull
Faeries 16, 26, 31, 32, 48, 57
Faggot 31
Fahan 24, 92
Fàlaire .... *See* Mare
Feamainn .... *See* Seaweed
Femen 17, 92
Fenius Farsaidh 3, 10, 13, 15,
   17, 19, 21, 23, 25, 27, 29, 31,
   33, 35, 37, 39, 41, 43, 45, 47,
   49, 51, 53, 55, 56, 57, 58
Fergus mac Róich 4
Fern 10, 17, 125
Fidba .... *See* Hedge-bill
Filideacht .... *See* Poetry
Final Ogham 83
Fine-colored 19
Finnen 17, 94
Fionn's Window 89, 90, 108, 109
Fionndruinne .... *See* Bronze
Fishing 51
Flail 39
Flann .... *See* Red
Fluting 31
Food Ogham 95
Foot Ogham 5, 95, 96
Fore-enclosed Ogham 71
Forfeda 10, 53, 61, 63, 65, 66, 96
Forfeda #1 65
Forfeda #2 65
Forfeda #3 66
Fortress Ogham 13, 92
Four-ridged Ogham of Crutine 80
Foursome Ogham 84
Fowling 49
Fox 19
Foyle 17, 92
Fraudulent Ogham 89

Fraxinus excelsior 21
Frog 15
Furze .... *See* Gorse
Gabor .... *See* Goat
Gabur 35, 93
Gaibneacht .... *See* Smithwork
Gat .... *See* Withe
Gavel 35, 92
Geanmchnù .... *See* Chestnut
Géis .... *See* Swan
George 35, 94, 141
Germania 6, 107, 108
Giorria .... *See* Hare
Goat 35
Gold 45
Goose 37
Gooseberry 57, 126
Gorm .... *See* Blue
Gormghlas .... *See* Aquamarine
Gorse 45, 46, 123, 126
Gort 35, 125
Graney 37, 92
Granite 49
Great Dotting Ogham 68
Green 37, 40
Grey 15, 27
Grianchloch .... *See* Quartz
Gull 17
Hadaig .... *See* Night Raven
Hamamelis mollis 58
Hammer 45
Handicraft 19
Hare 37
Harping 29
Hawk 19
Hawthorn 23, 125
Hazel 29, 122, 125
Head in Bush or Persisting
 Ogham 5, 77
Head of Dispute Ogham 69
Head on Proscription Ogham 83
Head Under Bush Ogham . 5, 77
Heather 47, 126
Heather- brush 47

Hedera helix 35
Hedge-bill 17
Hellebore 49
Hen 31
Herb Ogham 95
Herb trees 13, 33, 35, 37, 45,
 47, 57
Hinge Ogham 66
hOcha 24, 92
Holly 27, 28, 122, 125
Honeysuckle 56
Host Ogham 86
Hound 27, 29
Hound's Tounge 27
Huartan 24
Huath .... *See* Uath
hŮath .... *See* Uath
Hunt-track Ogham 82
Hyssop 51
Iach .... *See* Salmon
Iarann .... *See* Iron
Iascaireach .... *See* Fishing
Idad .... *See* Iodhadh
Idho .... *See* Iodhadh
Iduna 32
Ifín 57, 126
Ilex aquifolium 27
Illait .... *See* Eaglet
Indeoin .... *See* Anvil
Indiurnn 51, 92
Infilleted Ogham 69
Interwoven Thread Ogham 70
In Lebor Ogaim 3
Iodhadh 51, 126
Iodho .... *See* Iodhadh
Íosóip .... *See* Hyssop
Iphin .... *See* Ifin
Irfi nd .... *See* Very White
Irish Letter Names and Their
 Kennings 9, 21, 43
Iron 51
Islay 51, 93
Ita 51, 94
Ivy 35, 36, 125

Appendix 5 - A Word About Ár nDraíocht Féin

James, Simon 1
Kale 14
King Ogham 94
Lachu .... See Duck
Ladder Ogham of Fionn 78
Laisren 15, 94
Lamb 47
Lame Ogham 76
Land of the Ever Young 31
Lapwing 43
Lark 47
Lead 15
Leinster 1, 2, 3, 4, 6, 110, 141
Letter Rack Ogham 67
Liath .... See Grey
Liathlus .... See Mugwort
Lieschi 14
Liffy 15, 92
Livelihood 13
Lively Dotting Ogham 68
Loman .... See Rope
Lonicera xylosteum 56
Loscann .... See Frog
Lower Shannon 5, 15, 92
Luaidhe .... See Lead
Luamnacht .... See Pilotage
Luis 9, 10, 15, 125
Mac ind Óic 10, 13, 15, 17, 19, 21,
    23, 25, 27, 29, 31, 33, 35, 37,
    39, 41, 43, 45, 47, 49, 51, 53,
    55, 56, 57, 58
Mac Main, Morann 10, 13,
    15, 17, 19, 21, 23, 25, 27, 29,
    31, 33, 35, 37, 39, 41, 43, 45,
    47, 49, 51, 53, 55, 56, 57, 58
Machad 33
Mad Sweeney 11, 13,
    15, 17, 19, 21, 23, 25, 27, 29,
    31, 33, 35, 37, 39, 41, 43, 45,
    47, 49, 51, 53, 55
Madra Uisce .... See Otter
Mailp 59, 126
Malachite 33
Malaicít .... See Malachite

Malus sylvestris 31
Manchan 33, 94
Mane (?) Backwards Ogham . 85
Man (Human Being) Ogham 97
Maoildearg .... See Mulberry
Maple 59, 126
Mare 17
mBracht .... See Variegated
McManus, Damian 3, 9, 10
Meath 33, 93
Midir 6, 103
Milaideacht .... See Soldiering
Mintan .... See Titmouse
Mistletoe 25
Mixed Ogham 86
Modeling 37
Mouse colored 31
Mugwort 15
Muin 33, 111, 125
Muinten 33, 92
Mulberry 33
Munster 110
Nǽscu .... See Snipe
Nasc .... See Ring
Nathair .... See Adder
Nathartha .... See Serpentine
Naven 49, 93
Neantóg .... See Stinging Nettle
Neasan 21, 94
Necht .... See Clear
Nephin 21, 92
nGarman 37, 93
nGéadal 37, 125
nGéigh .... See Goose
nGeminus 37, 94
nGend .... See Wedge
nGetal. .... See nGéadal
nGibæ .... See Modeling
nGlas .... See Green
Night Raven 24
Nin .... See Nion
Nion 9, 21, 125
Nith 21, 92
Nóinín .... See Daisy

159

Norway Maple 59, 126
Nose Ogham 5, 95
Notaireacht ...... *See* Notary Work
Notary Work 21
Nuin .... *See* Nion
Oak 25, 125
Oblique Ogham 74
Odba 45, 93
Odhar .... *See* Dun
Odoroscrach .... *See* Scrat
Oena 45, 94
Ogham
   Abbreviations #1 Ogham . 63
   Abbreviations #2 Ogham . 63
   African Alphabet Ogham . 75
   Agricultural Ogham 13, 93
   Aliter Ogham 80
   Anguish of a Poet's Heart
     Ogham 67
   Arms Ogham 99
   Art Ogham 13, 94
   Bend (or Angle) Ogham ... 71
   Bird Ogham 5, 13, 93
   Blind Man Ogham 76
   Boat Ogham 100
   Boy Ogham 6, 62, 96
   Canal Ogham 79
   Church Ogham 93
   Coll Ogham 87
   Color Ogham 13, 93
   Combative Ogham 86
   Company Ogham 101
   Conjunct Ogham 82
   Corn-field Ogham 87
   Cow Ogham 98
   Diphthong Group Behind Us
     Ogham 78
   Dog Ogham 98
   Ebad-fashioned Ogham 67, 88
   Egyptian (Hebrew) Ogham 74
   Enclosed Ogham 68
   End to End Ogham 86
   Final Ogham 83

Fionn's Window . 89, 90, 108,
  109
Food Ogham 95
Foot Ogham 5, 95, 96
Fore-enclosed Ogham 71
Fortress Ogham 13, 92
Four-ridged Ogham of Crutine
  80
Foursome Ogham 84
Fraudulent Ogham 89
Great Dotting Ogham 68
Head in Bush or Persisting
  Ogham 5, 77
Head of Dispute Ogham .. 69
Head on Proscription Ogham
  83
Head Under Bush Ogham . 5,
  77
Herb Ogham 95
Hinge Ogham 66
Host Ogham 86
Hunt-track Ogham 82
Infilleted Ogham 69
Interwoven Thread Ogham 70
King Ogham 94
Ladder Ogham of Fionn ... 78
Lame Ogham 76
Letter Rack Ogham 67
Lively Dotting Ogham 68
Mane (?) Backwards Ogham
  85
Man (Human Being) Ogham
  97
Mixed Ogham 86
Nose Ogham 5, 95
Oblique Ogham 74
Ogham of Bricriu 80
Ogham of Erimon 70
Ogham of Fenius 88
Ogham that Confused Breas,
  Son of Elatha, The 82
Order Ogham 81
Ox Ogham 98
Palm of Hand Ogham .. 5, 96

Appendix 5 - A Word About Ár nDraíocht Féin

Pierced Ogham 72
Place Ogham 72
Point-to-eye Ogham 85
Ridgeless Ogham 69
River Pool Ogham . 5, 13, 92
Rope Ogham 71, 75
Saint Ogham 13, 94
Scandinavian Ogham 76
Secret Ogham of the Warrior bands 66
Separated Ogham 88
Serpent About Head Ogham 5, 77
Shield Ogham 73
Shin Ogham 5
Side Ogham of Tlachtga ... 70
Snake Through Heath Ogham 71
Sow Ogham 62, 96, 99
Stag Ogham 99
Strand Stream of Ferchertne Ogham 74
Stream Strand of Ferchertne 90
Strife Head Ogham 68
Three-stemmed Ogham of Fionn 79
Three Ridged Ogham 78
Tooth-like Ogham of Fionn 72
Twin Ogham 82
Two Stoke Ogham 87
Unnamed #1 Ogham 79
Unnamed #2 Ogham 81
Unnamed #3 Ogham 64
Unnamed #4 Ogham 101
Unnamed #5 Ogham 101
Unnamed #6 Ogham 68
Unnamed #7 Ogham 85
Unnamed #8 Ogham 69
Unnamed #9 Ogham 70
Unnamed #10 Ogham 71
Unnamed #11 Ogham 72, 75
Unnamed #12 Ogham 74
Unnamed #13 Ogham 75

Unnamed #14 Ogham 75
Unnamed of Ilann Ogham 66
Uproar of Anger Ogham .. 84
Viking Ogham #1 76
Viking Ogham #2 76
Water Ogham 97
Well-footed Ogham 70
Wheel Ogham of Roscadach 73
Woman Ogham 97
Word Ogham of Cuchullain 10
Word Ogham of Mac ind Óic 10
Word Ogham of Morann Mac Main 10
Ogham of Bricriu 80
Ogham of Dedu 68, 69
Ogham of Erimon 70
Ogham of Fenius 88
Ogham that Confused Breas, Son of Elatha, The 82
Ogma mac Elathan 3
Ogmoracht .... *See* Harvesting
Oinniún .... *See* Onion
Oir .... *See* Ór
Óisc .... *See* Sheep
Onion 45
Onn 45, 126
Or .... *See* Ór
Ór 55, 126
Ord .... *See* Hammer
Order Ogham 81
Osier Willow 19
Othain 24, 92
Otter 33
Ox 25, 98
Ox Ogham 98
Packsaddle 19
Palm of Hand Ogham 5, 96
Pan 35, 36
Peasant trees 13, 15, 17, 19, 23, 49
Phaeton 19
Phagos .... *See* Eamhancholl

161

Pheasant 5, 93
Phragmites australis 59
Piebald 43
Pierced Ogham 72
Piglet 24
Pilotage 15
Place Ogham 72
Plough 43
Poetry 17, 24
Point-to-eye Ogham 85
Populus alba 53
Populus tremula 49
Primrose 19
Prunis padus 60
Prunus spinosa 39
Quartz 37
Queirt .... *See* Ceirt
Querc .... *See* Hen
Quercus robur 25
Quert .... *See* Ceirt
Quiar. .... *See* Mouse colored
Quislenacht .... *See* Fluting
Red 17, 41, 49
Reed .... 37. *See also* Rush
Resinous 47
Ribes grossularia 57
Ridgeless Ogham 69
Ring 21
River Pool Ogham 5, 13, 92
Rócnat .... *See* Small Rook
Roigne 41, 93
Roisnin .... *See* Eyebright
Rón. .... *See* Seal
Ronnaireacht ..... *See* Dispensing
Rope 15
Rope Ogham 71, 75
Rowan 15, 125
Ruadh .... *See* Red
Ruadhan 41, 94
Ruby 41
Rúibín .... *See* Ruby
Ruis 41, 77, 126
Rusc .... *See* Basket
Rush 59, 126

Rye 41, 92
Sabhaircin .... *See* Primrose
Saighead 60
Sail 19, 125
Saille .... *See* Sail
Saint Ogham 13, 94
Sairsi .... *See* Handicraft
Salix viminalis 19
Salmon 51
Sambucus nigra 41
Scandinavian Ogham 76
Scholars' Primer, The 1
Scrat 45
Seal 41
Seanchus Mór 7
Seaweed 17
Secret Ogham of the Warrior-
  bands 66
Seg .... *See* Hawk
Seolae 19, 92
Separated Ogham 88
Serpentine 22
Serpent About Head Ogham .. 5, 77
Shannon 15, 19, 92
Sheep 45
Shield Ogham 73
Shin Ogham 5
Shrub trees 13, 39, 41, 53, 55, 56, 58
Side Ogham of Tlachtga 70
Silver 24
Silver Fir 43, 126
Sincheall 19, 94
Sionnach .... *See* Fox
Sloe. .... *See* Blackthorn
Small Rook 41
Smithwork 35
Snake Through Heath Ogham 71
Snipe 21
Sodath .... *See* Fine-colored
Soldiering 33
Sorbus aucuparia 15
Sorcha .... *See* Bright

Appendix 5 - A Word About Ár nDraíocht Féin

Sovereignty 43
Sow Ogham 62, 96, 99
Spás 60, 126
Spindle 55, 126
Srathar .... See Packsaddle
Sruthair 39, 92
Stag Ogham 99
Stail .... See Stallion
Stallion 39
Stan .... See Tin
Starling 27
Stinging Nettle 22
Stinólach .... See Thrush
Straif 39, 125
Straiph .... See Straif
Strand Stream of Ferchertne
  Ogham 74
Strannan 39, 94
Strawberry 39
Stream Strand of Ferchertne .. 90
Streghuindeacht See Deer-stalking
Streulae 39, 93
Strife Head Ogham 68
Suibhne Geilt 10, 143
Suíl Cat .... See Cat's Eye
Sulphur 39
Sust .... See Flail
Sú talún .... See Strawberry
Swan 35, 49
Sweet milk 95
Tacitus 6, 107, 108
Táin Bó Cuailnge 4
Tal .... See Adze
Taliesin 17, 114
Tara 4, 27, 92, 109
Taxus baccata 51
Teanga Cú .. See Hound's Tounge
Teith 27, 92
Temen .... See Dark Grey
Terrible 24
Three Ridged Ogham 78
Three-stemmed Ogham of Fionn
  79
Thrush 39

Tighearnach 27, 94
Tin 39
Tinne 27, 125
Titmouse 33
Tochmarc Étáine 6, 103
Tooth-like Ogham of Fionn ... 72
Topaz 27
Tópáz .... See Topaz
Torc .... See Boar
Tornoracht .... See Turning
Trefhocul 1, 141
Trisyllacic Poetry 24
Truith .... See Starling
Túatha Dé Danann 4, 16
Turning 27
Twin Ogham 82
Two Stoke Ogham 87
Uan .... See Lamb
Uath 23, 125
Uileand .... See Uilleann
Uilen .... See Uilleann
Uilleann 56, 66, 126
Uiseóg .... See Lark
Uissen 47, 92
Ulex europaeus 45
Ulster 110
Ultan 47, 94
Umaideacht .... See Brass work
Umha .... See Copper
Unach .... See Byrony
Unnamed #1 Ogham 79
Unnamed #2 Ogham 81
Unnamed #3 Ogham 64
Unnamed #4 Ogham 101
Unnamed #5 Ogham 101
Unnamed #6 Ogham 68
Unnamed #7 Ogham 85
Unnamed #8 Ogham 69
Unnamed #9 Ogham 70
Unnamed #10 Ogham 71
Unnamed #11 Ogham 72, 75
Unnamed #12 Ogham 74
Unnamed #13 Ogham 75
Unnamed #14 Ogham 75

Unnamed of Ilann Ogham 66
Uproar of Anger Ogham 84
Ur .... See Úr
Úr 47, 126
Ura .... See Úr
Usca .... See Heather-brush
Usgdha .... See Resinous
Usney 47, 93
Variegated 33
Very White 51
Viking Ogham #1 76
Viking Ogham #2 76
Vine 33, 35, 125
Vitus species 33
Voyage of Bran Mac Febal, The ... 4
Wagon 29
Water Ogham 97
Wedge 37
Well-footed Ogham 70
Wheel Ogham of Roscadach . 73
White 13, 51, 108
White Goddess, The ... 47, 51, 113, 114, 118
White Poplar 53, 54, 126
Willow 19, 115, 119, 122, 125
Witchhazel 58
Withe 35
Wizardry 25
Woman Ogham 97
Woodbine 56, 115, 121
Word Ogham of Cuchullain .. 10
Word Ogham of Mac ind Óic 10
Word Ogham of Morann Mac Main 10
Wren 25
Yarrow 24
Yellow Book of Lecan, The .. 1, 141
Yew 51, 126

About the Author

Rev. Robert Lee "Skip" Ellison

Rev. Skip Ellison started in the Neopagan movement when he was initiated into a Celtic Traditional Wiccian coven in 1982. In the fall of 1990, he had the opportunity to attend a workshop presented by Isaac Bonewits on Ár nDraíocht Féin, A Druid Fellowship (ADF).

Isaac's workshop interested him about ADF enough that he joined the organization soon after in 1990. He was mainly impressed by Isaac's vision of a religion that would be open to everyone, public and that, some day in the future, would have groves and temples in every city.

Since then, he has served on its Mother Grove beginning in 1992. He has held several positions and is currently ADF's Archdruid. He was the Grove Organizer for Muin Mound Grove, ADF in Syracuse, NY and became its second Senior Druid, a position he held until 2001, when he stepped down to become Archdruid of the International organization. He is currently in his third, and final, elected term as Archdruid.

He is a retired Industrial Electrician and now works at tending his land and gardens, learning more about history, and traveling around the US, Canada and Europe visiting ADF Groves and talking about ADF and other subjects at festivals.

He has authored five books titled: *The Wheel of the Year at Muin Mound Grove, ADF: A Cycle of Druid Rituals*, *The Druids' Alphabet: What Do We Know About the Oghams?*, *The Divine Liver - The Art and Science of Haruspicy as practiced by the Etruscans and Romans*, *The Solitary Druid: A Practitioner's Guide*, and *Ogham: The Secret Language of the Druids*.

He can be reached at skip@skipellison.us, or via his web site at http://www.skipellison.us/. Further information about his online classes and his books can also be found on the web site.

Made in the USA
Monee, IL
04 April 2025